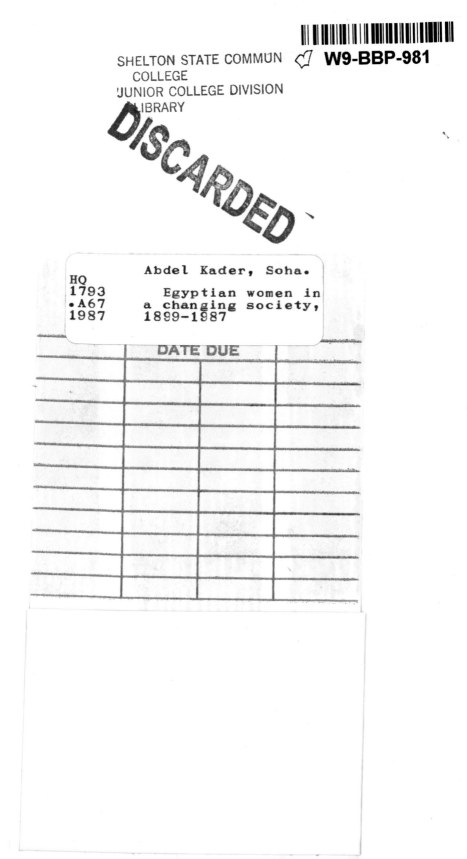

Egyptian Women in a Changing Society, 1899–1987

Mrs. Huda Sharawi,
Founder of the Egyptian Feminist Union

DISCARDED

Egyptian Women in a Changing Society, 1899–1987

Soha Abdel Kader
Social Research Center
The American University in Cairo

Lynne Rienner Publishers === Boulder & London

Published in the United States of America in 1987 by
Lynne Rienner Publishers, Inc.
948 North Street, Boulder, Colorado 80302

and in the United Kingdom by
Lynne Rienner Publishers, Inc.
3 Henrietta Street, Covent Garden, London WC2E 8LU

Library of Congress Cataloging-in-Publication Data

Abdel Kader, Soha.

   Egyptian women in a changing society, 1899-1987

   Bibliography: p.
   Includes index.
   1. Women—Egypt—Social conditions.   2. Women, Muslim
—Egypt—Social conditions.   3. Feminism—Egypt—History—
20th century.   I. Title.
HQ1793.A67   1987   305.4'2'0962   87-13234
ISBN 0-931477-47-6 (lib. bdg.)

Printed and bound in the United States of America

The paper used in this publication meets the
requirements of the American National Standard
for Permanence of Paper for Printed Library
Materials Z39.48-1984.   ∞

To the memory of my father,
Mohammed Zaki Abdel Kader

He once wrote:

Here I present models of women depicted from real life; models inspired by real women who strive among us and whom you may encounter anywhere. In some models, you will find a readiness to sacrifice that is almost saintly; in others, you will find a restlessness that almost amounts to decadence; but in all you will find both the throbbing of raw instinct and the loftiness of compassion. It is in the juxtaposition of raw instinct and lofty emotions that you will find women. But why do I say women?—you will find all human beings. (*Models of Women*, p. 1)

· Contents ·

· Photographs ·

· Preface ·

Writing on such an unwieldy topic as "women" is difficult. To progressives almost anything you write is not revolutionary enough, and to most traditionally-minded people, writing on women may seem either unnecessary or just plain asking for trouble. I see myself as a feminist, but only to the extent that I see women as discriminated against because of biological functions and erroneous assumptions as to their inherent traits. My support would equally go to the groups in any society—blacks, South Africans, Muslim Bulgarians, the proletariat—who are discriminated against and whose members are deprived of their rights as human beings to choose their destiny. I choose to write about Egyptian women because, being an Egyptian woman myself, this is the subject closest to my heart. I have grappled with it, turned it around in my mind, retrospected and introspected. Throughout, I have tried to keep my emotions in abeyance and to maintain my perspective; as most writers claim (although we invariably fail), I have been objective, I have reported facts as honestly and accurately as possible, and interpreted them, within the confines of the existing literature, as scientifically as possible.

Of the people who mold one's thoughts, it is impossible to draw a comprehensive list. My professors, both at the American University in Cairo and at Cairo University; women all over the world, who like myself have spent their lives writing on women, and whom I came to know through conferences, seminars, collaborative work, friendship, and correspondence; my colleagues and friends at the Social Research Center of the American University in Cairo; my father, to whom I dedicate this book; my husband, Mahmoud Kamel; my sons, Sherif and Seif—of each there is a part in this book.

There are professors, colleagues, and friends who have had a direct input. While I bear total responsibility for the final product (including any mistakes), I owe special thanks to:

Dr. Laila Shukry El-Hamamsy, Director of the Social Research Center—without her support and the facilities of the Social Research Center this book would not have appeared.;

Dr. Ali Dessouki, Director, Center for Political Studies, Cairo University; Dr. Earl Sullivan, Professor of Political Science, American University in Cairo; Dr. Fatma Khafaga, Program Officer for Women and Education, UNICEF Cairo Office—all three for promptly reading the initial manuscript, and for their laudable and critical comments.

Ms. Janice Murray, editor for Lynne Rienner Publishers—for reading the initial manuscript, asking astute questions, and copyediting the final manuscript.

Mrs. Bahiga Haikal, Director of the Social Research Center Library—for reading the initial manuscript, taking full responsibility for the bibliography, and bearing with me the burden of reference checking in the last rush of manuscript completion.

Mrs. Hekmat Wassef, Administrative Assistant at the Social Research Center, American University in Cairo—for being my first and most enthusiastic reader, and for bearing the total responsibility of repeated word processing for the several versions of each chapter and the completion of the final manuscript.

· Introduction ·

Arab women, like the countries to which they belong, have been little understood by researchers, who, until recently, have tended to treat women in the region as if they were one cohesive whole, homogeneous in all their needs and resources. In fact, the countries of the Arab world do share much in common. Islam, the Arabic language, customs, traditions, and geographic proximity are unifying factors. Islam (as a creed and religion), the Qoran, and the Prophet Muhammad's Hadiths, which are the sources of Islamic Sharia as well as of statutes governing marriage, divorce, inheritance, and so on, have been thought by many to be the major determinants of the status of Arab women, thereby circumscribing and prescribing their lives in ways that cut across country and class boundaries. Scholars have looked to the forces of tribal and family custom as unifying factors and have singled out the "traditional Arab family" as the aspect of Middle Eastern social organization that is the most fundamental, the most important, and the most resistant to change. The most obvious impact of the family, which is extended, patriarchal, patrilineal, and patrilocal, seems to be the social segregation between the sexes. This segregation is referred to as the "men's world and the women's world" or the public/private dichotomy. Because it is almost nonexistent outside the Middle East, the separation of the social worlds of men and women has attracted the attention of researchers since colonial times.

Although missionaries and explorers were responsible for most of this type of research, later sociologists also followed suit. A flood of sociological and anthropological studies of the Arab family made its appearance in the 1960s (Goode 1963:87–163). Cross-cousin and endogamous marriage patterns were the focus of research in most of these studies, which viewed women and the family synonymously. These studies concerned themselves with the veiling and seclusion of women, the high value placed on their virginity before marriage, and their chastity within marriage.

Yet it soon became clear that to speak of Arab women as an entity was open to debate. Beneath the overall but rather thinly spread veneer of Islam and local custom and tradition, the culture of the Arab region is a complex mosaic that is intricately structured, both horizontally and vertically. Historical developments and local economic, political, and social factors distinguish each country of the region. The rate of social change and modernization, or more specifically, "Westernization," has been different in each country and within each country's social strata. The early explorers and sociologists who studied Arab women did not take into account individual differences, social and economic differences, or rural-urban differences among the women of the region. By using imported models and imported methodology that ignored the structural and dynamic aspects of the societies in question, these researchers undermined their understanding of indigenous cultures and of the true conditions of women in these cultures. Because most researchers were men and foreign, they had little opportunity to talk to or know women in any meaningful fashion (Rassam 1984a).

Until the early 1970s, multiregional studies, both sociological and missionary, in answering only questions that transcended cultural boundaries produced no more than a static, idealized caricature of Arab women. Useful only for a general understanding of the condition of women, these studies reinforced and fed one of two stereotyped images—Arab women as exotic odalisques dedicated to the sensual pleasures of men, or Arab women as "beasts of burden" born and reared for childbearing, charged with arduous chores, and subjected to all forms of exploitation inside and outside the home (Rassam 1984). However, during the 1970s, several pioneering female ethnographers from within the region and from outside it redefined research questions, reformulated research methodology, conducted more in-depth research, and brought to the fore the misrepresentation of the reality of Arab women in the existing body of literature.

A major aspect of the lifeless caricature of Arab women that was challenged through the accumulation of more realistic and specific information on their roles and lifestyles was the public/private dichotomy, for long a leitmotif of the literature on Arab women. Studies of Arab societies, in examining the existence of two separate and sharply differentiated social worlds for men and women, had defined the public world of men as that of politics, religion, and the market and the private world of women as that of the home. Implicit in this dichotomy of public/male, private/female was the assumption that power, which according to this view belonged to the public/political domain, was the monopoly of men and that women, because they were confined to the private sphere, therefore were powerless. The recent work of female ethnographers on women in Muslim societies was most invaluable in correcting this all too rigid and formalistic conception of earlier scholars (see, for example, Nelson 1973). By advocating a redefinition of power to encompass how men and women are involved in negotiating their social orders, these later ethnographers demonstrated that there was a reciprocity of influence between men and women and that the segregation of the sexes did not necessarily mean the subordination of women. This research showed that Arab women wielded power in a variety of ways, including the use of the veil as a means to express themselves; Arab women mediated conflicts, were involved in arranging marriages, and were by no means as "powerless" or as submissive as earlier scholars assumed.

Despite attempts to rectify the biases of previous stereotyped images, a dominant characteristic of the literature on Arab women remains the singling out of Islam as the most important factor determining their status (Abdel Kader 1984). This is partially a reflection of the state of the art of Middle Eastern history, which in bearing the imprint of "orientalism" has tended to tie students of the Middle East, historians, and others to the written word. This has resulted in a specifically "Islamic" definition of history that affects sources and methodology. Consequently, most historians and researchers have shied away from exploring the wider social, economic, and political realities and have limited themselves to the confines of the text of the Qoran and the Hadiths (Tucker 1983). To this day, the bulk of the literature on women in the Arab region, in both Arabic and foreign languages, centers on the eternally controversial issue of whether Islam raised or lowered the status of women in the region (Al-Qazzaz 1977). The available literature is divided into two broad categories: studies that adopt a *defensive posture* (that Islam sustains rather than undermines women's rights) and studies that adopt a *critical posture* (that Islam is to blame for the "low" status of women and the inequality of the sexes prevalent in the Muslim world).

The defenders of the position of women in Islam argue that although the Qoran and the Prophet's original teachings at the present time may seem to subjugate women, an examination of the lifestyle prevalent during Muhammad's time indicates loose family ties, predominant polygamy, easy divorce and remarriage, and an obsession with sexual pleasure. Pre-Islamic institutions, particularly female infanticide and marriage by kidnapping, were highly unfavorable to women. In this respect, the Prophet's rulings in fact were directed toward improving the quality of life for both men and women. Islamic institutions, particularly of the Utopian Age of Islam during the seventh century, elevated the status of women by banning female infanticide, limited to four the number of women a man could marry, and imposed adequate provisions by the husband for his wife and children within marriage and even after divorce (see, for example, Culver 1967; Levy 1965; Yusef 1965; Saleh 1972).

The critics of the status of women in Islam argue that in essence the

Qoran offers no real ethical codes or moral values regarding male-female relations. The enjoyment of physical pleasures, particularly for men, is accepted and accommodated. Women, on the other hand, are primarily sexual objects to be protected from their own immoral qualities and hidden behind veils and curtains. Muslim marriage is based on the premise that social order can be maintained only if a woman's dangerous potential for chaos is restrained. Women thus are held as a prize piece of property, not as persons. A new sexual order and new legislation are needed to remove the limitations to women's potential (see, for example, Bousquet 1966; Bullough 1973; Mernissi 1975).

That Islam has bettered the lives of Muslim women or that Islam has made of them "the serfs of the modern world" is both true and false depending on how, when, where, and who interprets the precepts of Islam. Every great intellectual and moral tradition can bear numerous interpretations. This is true of liberalism, socialism, Marxism, and it also is true of Christianity, Judaism, and Islam. Yet studying how their precepts are expounded in any specific community is more important than studying the ideological precepts of these intellectual and moral traditions. Islam as practiced in Egypt or Iraq is quite different from the Islam practiced in Algeria, and it is certainly not the Islam practiced in Senegal, Indonesia, or among the Hausa of Nigeria. In dealing with Islam, we are not dealing with one Islam, but with Islams, and even pseudo-Islams.

Past studies already have indicated the presence of a coherent and dominant ideology concerning female sexuality in Islamic thought. Sexuality in the Arab world, like elsewhere, is a basic component of self-identity. The ideological definitions of the status and roles of women in the Qoran and the Hadiths cannot be ignored. However, an examination of the textual formulations of these ideological definitions is less revealing (in the present context) than is an investigation of how they are internalized, interpreted, and practiced by Muslim men and women in each country.

Studies of women in the history of Arab countries, few as these studies are, also have contributed their share of skewed images. Most of these studies focus on the "famous women" in the Arab past to the exclusion of all other classes of women (Abdel Kader 1984); this, too, reflects the state of the art of Middle Eastern historiography. Long after historians in Europe and other parts of the world had embarked on studies of social and economic history, Middle Eastern historians remained confined to studying visible political institutions, diplomatic events, and the intellectual currents of high, as opposed to popular, culture. The accessibility to resources on the literate, powerful, and influential and the view that what is of value in the study of a culture is limited to the norms and formal prescriptions of the few who hold authority encouraged this concentration on the formal domains of politics and economy. This effectively meant that all but upper-class males were left out of the historical process. Women, along with many other societal groups and classes, were relegated to a minor and peripheral place in history (Tucker 1983).

Only women who participated in elite politics and male-dominated culture receive attention in historical studies. Most history books on Arab women are biographical sketches that demonstrate the exemplary virtues of such prominent "early Muslim women" as Khadija, first wife of the Prophet Muhamed, Aisha Bint Bakr, his last wife, and Fatima, his sole surviving child. The underlying assumption, sometimes implicit and sometimes explicit, in these studies is that these "great women of the ancient Middle East" should serve as worthy examples for modern women. The "great feats" these great women accomplished nullify the view that men alone were created for leadership in politics, war, and building civilizations and prove that the seclusion and confinement of Arab women in modern times are arbitrary and extra-Islamic measures. Yet, worthy as these messages are, such studies only reinforce and emphasize the peripherality and marginality of the majority of women to a true understanding of culture and the historical process. These messages also promote the view that women are important only when they join the public domain. The domain of the home, to which rigid conceptual formulations have assigned women, remains insignificant and of little value.

A few historical studies address themselves to the lives and history of Arab women in the nineteenth and twentieth centuries. The aim of these studies is to highlight the contrast between the "traditional" and changing "modern" worlds of Arab women (Badran 1979). Sharing the idealist bent of Middle Eastern history as a whole, most of the studies perceive the changes in the roles and status of Arab women as a product of the transfer of Western ideas. Implicit in this analysis is the assumption that Arab women were doomed to an unchanging oppression dictated by the Qoran and Hadiths, or by customs and traditions, and that this oppression only began to lift in the nineteenth century with the coming of Western thought.

Interest in social and economic history has risen dramatically in the Middle East. Several pioneering works utilizing theories and approaches developed in other disciplines are making their appearance. Yet, even in these works, women are largely ignored and given only cursory treatment. Some authors lament the dearth of information on women, but on the whole and with a few exceptions, the social history of the Middle East is being written without women (Tucker 1983).

After decolonization, most governments of the region came to view rapid socioeconomic development as a major goal. Empirical studies of the roles and status of women acquired particular interest because of the overriding concern with socioeconomic development and the necessity of integrating women in its processes. The rise of Arab socialism in the 1950s and its fuller growth in the 1960s also gave a strong impetus to this type of research, which was inspired by statist goals of equality for women or by Marxist ideology. The a priori assumption underlying many of the studies of this type is that Arab women's roles in social production, especially in wage labor, are the key to their past and future. As empirical indices of their status and as catalysts for their liberation, the increased enrollment of Arab women in all levels of education, their increased participation in the labor force, and their acquisition of new political and labor rights are the focus of these studies.

However, these studies, valuable and optimistic as they are, are based on ideas extrinsic to Arab society and neglect the specificity of Arab history, social organization, and culture. Official state policy is given central importance, while indigenous forces that acted and continue acting to encourage or impede Arab women's participation in social production are neglected. Such studies, written from the perspective of a modernization theory or of Marxism, emphasize some aspects of the lives of Arab women at the cost of others. More often than not, the data focus on Westernized women who form a minority that is not representative of the majority of women in the region.

Understanding the position of women in Arab-Islamic countries is not a problem sui generis. It partakes of the problem of understanding women in any society. No one factor, be it Islam, local custom and tradition, or Westernization, can explain the position of Arab women. As mentioned earlier, whether Islam has bettered or lowered the status of Arab women remains an issue of strong debate. That local custom and tradition have circumscribed the lives of many women is true, but it also is true that they have fought back and found means and ways to impose their wishes and desires, often paying no more than lip service to those of their male masters. That Westernization has changed the lives of Arab women is true, but it has changed the lives of only a few women from the urban upper strata who in consequence became even more marginal and peripheral to their societies. As "models" for change these emancipated women have remained rejected, neglected, or at best considered unreachable.

Defining the roles and status of Arab women is no easy task. There can be no "final word" on the matter. Their roles, status, and lifestyles are not static or unchanging, but have been as dynamic and mutable as the societies to which they belong. Women's roles have fluctuated historically, do continue to fluctuate, and will fluctuate in the future. Further, these roles and status were never isolated or independent phenomena but were a function, at any one point in history, of the interrelationship between a multiplicity of social, economic, and political factors. The very intricacy of the interrelationship among these factors and the specific ways in which it affects the lives of all people, whether male or female, adult or child, rich or poor, more often than not defies understanding. This is partly because of the insufficiency of data and the failure to ask the appropriate questions, but also is due in part to the complexity of life itself.

Understanding the position of women in Arab societies is especially problematic because of the paucity of data. Given the status of research on women in the region, we still are very far from being able to formulate some grand theory that would interpret and explain women's status across time and place. The paucity of comparable data on Arab women precludes the emergence of an encompassing theory that could explain the varying status found among Bedouin women, peasant women, and the urban elite, for example. This is especially true for a society as enormous, complex, and with as long and rich a history as the Arab world. What the status of research on women in the Arab world amounts to is that we have *some* knowledge about *some* aspects of women's lives in *some* parts of the region for *some* strata and during *some* periods of history (Van Dusen 1976). As a leading Arab social scientist in the field has noted, "We are still at the stage of exploring the tip of the iceberg: much remains hidden" (Rassam 1984b:122).

Methodology is inseparable from the elements that precede it and follow it in the thought process; thus, methodology is inseparable from epistemology—that is, from the ideology and vision of the world that shape the research efforts, the techniques, and the means selected for data collection (Lucas 1983). In seeking to generate new data on women and women's history, we cannot avoid confronting all the questions involved from the initial stages to the final stage of the research process. Without a theoretical framework that recognizes the intricate relation of women's roles and status to the economic, political, and social organization of society, the accumulation of more data may be haphazard and futile.

Yet, focusing on understanding the position of Arab women is neither feminist chauvinism nor superfluous intellectualism. Studying women in any society is not a peripheral or complementary undertaking, but is an integral part of understanding that culture. The activities and status of women, at any one point in time, reflect and affect the socioeconomic and political factors prevalent in the larger society. Our field of inquiry must be expanded to include these roles, status, and lifestyles, as well as those of men, if we hope to achieve true understanding of any cultural system.

• EGYPTIAN WOMEN IN A CHANGING SOCIETY, 1899–1987 •

Egyptian women share many of the characteristics and face many of the same problems as women in other Arab-Islamic countries. When Egypt was conquered by the Arabs in 640 A.D. and thus came under the influence of Islam, this had a profound effect on women's roles and status. Egypt remained under the influence of the Arabs for many centuries. Although all historical accounts point to the fact that women in the early days of Islam in Arabia and the countries that came under the influence of the Arabs played an active role in the social and political life of the community, in later periods the mis-interpretation of the Qoran and other Islamic literature led to the deteriora-tion of family life and of the lives of women. This was particularly true during the time of the Turks. Egypt came under the rule of the Turks and part of the Ottoman Empire in 1517; the Turks' exaggerated, formal interpretation of the Qoran, especially its clauses relating to women, resulted in the issuing of a large number of administrative edicts oppressive to them. Turkish women led very secluded and passive lives, and this became the lot of Egyptian women for several centuries and up to the end of the nineteenth century (Abdel Kader 1973).

This does not mean, however, that Egyptian women have lived in a time-less, privatized world untouched by historical change. The continued re-definition and reassessment of the roles and status of women have been one of the most distinctive features of Egypt's modern history. A review of this history attests to the fact that the most dramatic changes in the reassessment and redefinitions of these roles and status have occurred during those mo-ments when the country itself was passing through social, political, or eco-nomic crisis (Nelson 1984:223–224). The British occupation of 1882 and the consequent 1919 revolution, the 1952 revolution and 1967 defeat, the Oc-tober War of 1973, and the initiation of the *infitah* (open-door) economic policies in 1974 have been important periods of transition in the history of the country as well as important landmarks in the history of the Egyptian feminist movement.

The beginnings of reassessment of the roles and status of Egyptian women occurred in the nineteenth century within the context of the Islamic Reform Movement. The works of reformers like Muhammad Abdu, Gamal al-Din al-Afghani, and others kept the discussion of the position of women in society, marriage, and the family an integral part of the ongoing reformist intellectual debate throughout the century. However, it remained for Qasim Amin, an Egyptian lawyer and jurist, to make this field of inquiry his own. Amin devoted an entire book to the issue; *The Emancipation of Women,* published in 1899, identified him as the first Egyptian and Arab feminist. The book was attacked from every conservative quarter, raising an extended and heated debate, and it transformed the "woman question" into a full-fledged feminist movement.

Since then, the Egyptian feminist movement has passed through several distinctive phases. Although the periodization of history is always arbitrary, I have identified five phases through which the Egyptian feminist movement has passed, each phase coinciding with important periods of transition in Egyptian history. These five phases are the intellectual debate phase (1899–

pre–World War I); the nationalist phase (1919–1924); the social activism phase (1924–1950s); the statist socialist phase (1952–1970s); and the *infitah* phase (1970s–present). The emergence of each phase was the outcome of a convergence of political, economic, and social factors that brought about an eruption of demands for change in the position of women. Another set of factors converged to bring about the decline of each phase and its transformation into the next. The delineation of the characteristics of each phase and the factors that led to its emergence and then its decline and transformation forms the core of this book.

The literature on Egyptian women is extensive. More has been written about them than about women in any other Arab country. Yet, much of the available literature, whether in Arabic or foreign languages, suffers from the same biases and shortcomings as does the literature on Arab women: generalization, reductionism, textualism, and elitism. Additions to our limited store of knowledge on the history and present situation of women in Egypt remains a vital task of empirical research. Studies of the ideological definitions of women's position must be supplemented by careful research on the actual position of women in the various periods of Egyptian history.

This book does not purport to rectify the biases and shortcomings of former research. Far from it. Although written within a theoretical framework that recognizes the intricate relationship of women's roles and status to the social, economic, and political organization of society, given the paucity of empirical data and its reliance, for the most part, on secondary sources, this is an exploratory study. Also, given that the impact of social change on the roles and status of women is a complex, multidimensional phenomenon that cannot be conceptualized easily, this book's approach is eclectic and multidisciplinary. A number of theoretical approaches and conceptual frameworks have been advanced to explain and understand women's status. These have been used according to the period of Egyptian history under investigation and the socioeconomic and political ramifications of this period for the corresponding phase of the Egyptian feminist movement.

One further bias in the research on Arab women has been the tendency to treat them in a theoretical and contextual vacuum. It is as if Muslim women represent a species apart, their lives and roles subject to unique laws and imperatives (Rassam 1984b). Although the experiences of Arab women need not mirror those of women in other parts of the world in all details, there is little reason to doubt the similarity in overall trends. There are structural, institutional, and ideological differences between the so-called developed and developing countries. Yet, there are similarities in women's grievances and demands that cut across country and time boundaries. There also are similarities in the social, economic, and political conditions that at one point in time produce an eruption of a feminist movement or raise voices demanding change.

On another level of analysis this book aims to place the Egyptian feminist movement in a more international and comparative perspective. Undertaking such a task would have been impossible a decade ago. There simply was not enough information. Many people have tried to explain why feminist movements emerged, what they wanted, and how—or whether— they achieved their aims. Almost invariably these investigators have based their explanation on one country. It is only by looking at feminism in a variety of countries that we can overcome this distortion in perspective and reach a more comprehensive grasp of the history of efforts to "emancipate" women and change their roles and status in society. Several books and articles that made their appearance during the past decade have tried to do just that. Although mostly on Western, particularly U.S. feminism, this work has been invaluable for the present analysis.

Elise Boulding (1976), in her monumental work, *The Underside of History: A View of Women Through Time,* realized that history is a problem of sampling and that our understanding of women in history suffers from a triple bias: a male bias, a class bias, and a Western bias.

> Anyone wandering in the bookstores of Stockholm, Brussels, Frankfurt, or Chicago looking for history books will find hundreds on the history of Western civilization, and only dozens on the history of the rest of the world. Yet most of the human beings who have walked through history have lived elsewhere. . . . It would not matter so much that those of us who live in the West focus on our own recent history, if we keep it in its proper perspective. But, of course we do not. . . . The elimination of most of the human race from the historical records shrinks our human identity. We don't know fully who we are. We know even less what we might become (pp. 3–4).

• DEFINITION OF CONCEPTS •

Broadly, the purpose of this book is to study the impact of social change on the status and roles of Egyptian women. More specifically, the aim is to study Egyptian feminism as a social movement. I have not selected one theory of social change or social movements and tried to apply it rigidly. Rather, I have borrowed conceptual frameworks to facilitate discussions and the presentation of ideas and to arrive at empirical generalizations I discuss fully in the conclusions. Within this context, the definitions of status, role, social movements, and feminism I am adopting in this book are as follows: *Status* usually refers to "an individual's place in social structure, i.e. in a graded order of power, rank or esteem" (Buvinic 1976:1). With reference to women, status usually means their ranking in the existing social structure *in comparison* to men. The most frequently used empirical indicators of the status of women are their proportions to total membership in the labor force and to total enrollment in the different educational levels as well as women's position in legal codes (constitutions, labor laws, family laws, and so on). There are those who argue against these empirical indices of the status of women because these measures only show women's status within the "formal" power structures, while women have been found to wield most of their power outside such structures. Yet, for lack of better empirical indices, I have drawn, where appropriate, on existing empirical and statistical indices.

Role usually refers to what an individual does as the occupant of a certain status; more specifically role is "the expected behavior associated with a particular social position" (Buvinic 1976:5). The correspondence between status and role is quite complex and indeed far from perfect. Theoretically, changes in the one should entail changes in the others. Yet, in reality this is not always so or at least there is a time lag between changes in the one and corresponding changes in the other. In my analysis of the different phases of Egyptian feminism, I have identified phases when the emphasis was on changing both the status and roles of women (the intellectual debate phase), when their roles changed but their status did not (the nationalist phase), and when women's status changed but their roles remained significantly the same (the statist socialist phase). The correspondence between the status and roles of Egyptian women and the reasons for the differential changes in both or either are discussed within the relevant chapters.

Religion the world over is an important source for ideological definitions of both the status and roles of women, and this is certainly so for Egyptian and Arab women. However, I take the precepts of the Islam as defined in the Qoran and the Prophet's Hadiths as a common denominator and a given. Although their ideological definitions of the status and roles of Egyptian women loom large in the background, my emphasis is on the contextual realities (social, economic, and political factors) that during the different phases of Egyptian history and the Egyptian feminist movement have forced redefinitions and reassessments of women's status and roles. These reassessments and redefinitions sometimes move the roles and status of women closer to those traditionally assumed to be prescribed by Islam; sometimes Islam recedes in the background, and more secular definitions are adopted.

The study of social movements and their interrelationship with social change is a broad, multidisciplinary field of research with many different schools of thought and many approaches. A major shift in emphasis during the past two decades from the older schools of collective behavior and mass psychology (Gustare le Bon, Gabriele Tarde, and Sigmund Freud) has been to view human beings acting collectively as "creators" rather than as "creatures" of social change (Oberschall 1973). The shift has been from emphasis on the irrationality, spontaneity, and emotional contagion of "collective behavior" to the role of "collective behavior" as an integral part of the normal operation of society and as an expression of the broader processes of social change. Within the context of this new approach, collective behavior, even though at times spontaneous, also can be organized and conscious behavior that gives rise to new perspectives, new values, new lines of action, and new institutions. Joseph Gusfield, a member of the Chicago/Parke School of Collective Behavior, first drew attention to the role played by social movements in the development of social change by defining them as "socially shared demands for change in some aspect of the social order" and as having "the character of an explicit and conscious indictment of whole or part of the social order, with a conscious demand for change" (Gusfield 1968:445).

At the base of every social movement there is a situation of social conflict, which is defined by Coser as "a struggle over values or claims to status, power and scarce resources" (1967:232). Anthony Obschall (1973:33) argues that social conflict arises from the very fact of social organization—that is, the structured arrangement of individuals and groups in a social system. In every social organization some positions are entrusted with a right to exercise control over other positions. In other words, there is a division of authority; some groups and individuals are subject to authority while others are participants in the exercise. In every social system there also is a division of labor through which the satisfaction of individual wants and the provision of collective goods are pursued. This structured societal arrangement creates complex relationships of exchange among the social positions, strata, and classes of the social system and results in a complex configuration of relations of domination and subordination. Thus, those in a dominant position have a vested interest in conserving and consolidating the status quo, and those in a subordinate position have a vested interest in changing that same status quo. Social conflict arises from the clash between these opposing interests.

With the a priori assumption, and despite some arguments to the contrary, that women as a social group in most societies of the world occupy a position of subordination and men as a social group occupy positions of dominance, one can argue safely that within most societies there is always a potential situation of social conflict. However, for every situation of social conflict there are number of accelerating and delaying factors that affect the timing of the eruption of conflict and its emergence into a social movement. My focus in the ensuing chapters has been to delineate and identify these factors.

The selection of a definition of feminism as a conceptual framework poses more serious problems. First, as an aside, but a significant aside, there is no equivalent to the term *feminism* in the Arabic language. The *Oxford English-Arabic Dictionary of Current Usage* (Doniach 1972) translates feminist as "someone who advocates equal rights for men and women" and feminism as "the belief in the equality of the sexes." There is no single Arabic word or words to signify either meaning. The fact in itself is indicative of the place feminism occupies in contemporary Arabic thought. Other schools of thoughts such as liberalism, communism, or democracy have found their way into the Arabic language either in transliteration or translation. But drawing on definitions of feminism in non-Arabic literature opens up a Pandora's box. Like the many faces of Eve, feminism has appeared in different guises in the same country during the same or different periods, and it also has meant different things in different countries.

Broadly, the essential idea of feminism in its usual current English usage is "the doctrine of equal rights for women, based on the theory of the equality of the sexes." Yet, the idea of the equality of sexes in any language is far from clear. There are feminist writers who deny that women are in any way inferior to men and instead believe that women and men have very different natures with very different needs. Thus, these writers justify the traditional dichotomy of public and private domains by which the public domain of economic and political society with its appropriate rights is reserved to men, while the private domain of home and family is reserved to women. There are feminist writers who go beyond equality of the sexes and argue for the natural superiority of women. Believing that motherhood, childbearing, and childrearing are of far greater social and moral value than any other social, economic, or political activity, these theorists advocate the subjugation of men to women and even indulge in the fantasy of totally doing away with men (see, for example, Solanis 1967).

Perhaps a more adequate formulation of the basic idea of equality of the sexes is one that sees women as having "equal worth" to men in respect of their common nature as free persons. According to this definition, there is no difference between men and women in terms of their fundamental worth. There are no male beings and female beings, but only human beings or persons. The nature and value of persons are independent of gender. In this formulation equality does not mean that all human beings have the same mental and physical capacities. Whether or not some are mentally or physically superior to others is irrelevant to the validity of their claims to equal worth. This claim means that as free beings individuals are capable of directing themselves to ends of their own choosing and that with respect to this capacity for self-direction, individuals have the same worth. This is the definition of feminism forwarded by John Charvet (1982:2–3) in the introduction to his book *Feminism,* and it is the definition that comes closest to formulating my own stance when it comes to the perennial question of male/female relations in society.

Beyond the concept of equality, feminist theorists have coined new terms to qualify the different genres of feminism that have emerged throughout the history of feminist movements in the Western world. The categorizations of the genres of feminism have been based on two criteria: ideological origins and aims or goals. In terms of ideological roots, "individualist feminism," for example, qualifies feminism that emanated from the eighteenth century Age of Enlightenment in Europe; "evangelical feminism" refers to feminism that owes its intellectual origins to the concepts of motherhood, family, and evangelicalism; "socialist feminism," as part of socialist doctrine, views women as only one of the many oppressed groups in society; and "radical feminism" views the institution of patriarchy as a very special form of oppression and not just one of the many forms of oppression (Evans 1977; Banks 1981). In terms of aims and programs, theorists distinguish between "social feminism"—that is, feminism that considers the struggle for women's rights as part of broader social reform movements—and "hard-core feminism," whose basic goal is the acquisition of suffrage rights for women (O'Neill 1969). A very narrow formulation of feminism has been termed "domestic feminism," which is feminism that advocates that women should be paid for housework.

For the purposes of my own analysis and as a general conceptual framework, I have chosen to use feminism in its broadest possible sense to mean any demands for change in the position of women. Any groups or individuals who have tried to change the position of women or change ideas about women have been granted the title of feminists, and their actions and thoughts have been termed feminism. This definition, forwarded by Banks (1981:3–4), seems more suitable for analyzing Egyptian feminism than a narrower definition or a definition that specifies equality of the sexes because the former allows inclusion of all relevant groups and phases. Egyptian feminism has not been, by any means, one unified movement, and its demands and dimensions have not been the same throughout its short history. A narrower definition of feminism that stresses equality would have effectively meant leaving out significant groups and phases, particularly the *infitah* phase where there has been a resurgence of Islamic fundamentalism and an almost total rejection of the concept of "equality" for the sexes.

• ORGANIZATION OF THE BOOK •

This book consists of three parts. The take-off point is the year 1899—which is the year of the publication of Qasim Amin's book *The Emancipation of Women*. Part 1, consisting of one chapter, therefore is an analysis of the roles and status of the different classes of Egyptian women at the end of the nineteenth century. Although throughout the book I draw mainly on secondary sources, I was lucky to be allowed access to the private memoirs of a member of my family. Given the paucity of primary sources, I felt it of value to incorporate an analysis of these memoirs in Chapter 1. Aside from this, Chapter 1 draws mostly on secondary sources. Part 2 of the book consists of five chapters, corresponding to the five phases of the Egyptian feminist movement outlined previously. Part 3 presents conclusions.

· PART ONE ·

The Beginnings of Egyptian Feminism

Qasim Amin (1863–1908), who was dubbed the "Liberator of Egyptian Women"
(Photograph courtesy of al-Akhbar*)*

CHAPTER ONE

Egyptian Women at the End
of the Nineteenth Century

The most visible class of women in chronicles of nineteenth century Egypt are *hareem* women. Belonging exclusively to the urban upper classes, these women constituted perhaps no more than 2 percent of Egypt's 5 million female population. Yet, historians and other researchers alike have tended to generalize from *hareem* women to the majority of Egyptian women, and we have been told repeatedly that Egyptian women at the turn of the century led idle, secluded, circumscribed, and veiled lives within the confines of their homes.

There may be some justification behind this tendency to generalize from the lives of upper-class *hareem* women to the lives of all Egyptian women. That Egypt is, and has been throughout history, an authoritarian society is a well-established fact. Societies dependent on irrigated agriculture are highly centralized, and Egypt has been such a society from time immemorial. Egypt was the first civilization in ancient history to develop a centralized government. This age-old reliance on a central authority has affected both formal and informal power structures and has led to the development of a society that is highly stratified both horizontally and vertically. *Hareem* women, even though numerically insignificant, in a hierarchical society where what the elite did was considered an ideal by other strata loomed very large on a symbolic level.

Yet it is now commonly accepted that when we speak of women in any society, we are not speaking of a uniform, homogeneous group. As women's status, roles, and lifestyles differ from one society to the next, they also differ from one socioeconomic class to the other. How then did the different classes of women fare at the turn of the century in Egypt? This chapter commences with a discussion of the lifestyle of *hareem* women at the end of the nineteenth century, then proceeds, within the confines of existing literature, to a discussion of the lifestyles of other classes of Egyptian women. The chapter also includes a presentation of a number of indices of the status and roles of women during the same period.

• *HAREEM* WOMEN •

Descriptions of the lives of *hareem* women, whether in Egypt or elsewhere in the Arab-Islamic world, have been stereotypical. The word *hareem* comes from the Arabic word *haram,* meaning "sanctuary" or "holy place." The Kaba in Mecca is *haram* because as a sanctuary anyone who seeks refuge in it is immune to violence or pursuit. *Haram* also means "the forbidden." This dualistic aspect gave rise to *hareem,* which primarily means the separate quarters for women within the household, or the women themselves and their children (Yehia 1983:29–34). However, historians, especially Western historians, generally associate the institution of *hareem* with polygamy and concubinage and thus tend to depict *hareems* as "lascivious places where odalisques recline in voluptuous poses in expectation of their masters' visits" (Marsot 1978:25).

No doubt these descriptions do apply to the royal *hareem* of the sultanate of the Ottoman Empire, of which Egypt became a part in 1517. Turkish caliph/sultans, besides issuing a large number of administrative edicts oppressive to women, also were responsible for developing *hareem* as an institution that embodied and was organized around the notion that women were sex objects and nothing more (Ahmed 1984:202). The royal *hareem* in Constantinople contained a multitude of female slaves and eunuch-guards, as well as an assortment of women chosen for their beauty and destined for the pleasure and service of the sultan. These women were organized in a pyramidal form. At the base of the pyramid were the novices (*sagridelar*), and at the top were the few favorites of the sultan (*ikbale*).

However, *hareem* as it came to be known in Egypt, whether in the ruling Mohammad Ali royal Turkish family, among wealthy Turks residing in Egypt, or among wealthy Egyptians, was only a miniature and "tasteless" imitation of the *hareem* of the sultanate of the Ottoman Empire (Yehia 1983:29–34). Although the royal *hareem* in Constantinople had inherited all the luxury and glory of the Byzantine Empire, Egyptian *hareems* had none of this. This was especially true by the end of the nineteenth century, for two reasons.

First, the British occupation of Egypt in 1882, inadvertently brought about by the Orabi Revolt and the precarious condition of the country's finances, entailed a change in class structure. Before the advent of the British, Turks were the most important landowners, owing to the fact that the ruling dynasty was Turkish and that large land grants had been given to the Turks in Egypt. They also occupied all administrative official ranks above village headman, or *shaikh al-balad,* as well as all commanding posts in the army. Because of a similarity of religion and cultural background, there was considerable social intermingling and intermarriage among Turks and upper-class Egyptians so that the highest echelon of society consisted of the Turkish-Egyptian aristocracy. After the British occupation, Egypt remained under the sovereignty of the Ottoman Empire, and Khedive Tawfiq was succeeded in 1882 by Khedive Abbas Helmi II as the local representative of Sultan/Caliph Abdul Hamid in Constantinople. However, the virtual ruler of Egypt from 1882 to 1907 was Lord Cromer, the British agent and consul-general. The British thus came to replace Turks in all commanding administrative and army posts. Furthermore, except for the ruling Mohammad Ali family, Turks also lost their status as the largest and most important landowners. The loss of political power by Turks was accompanied by a decline in their position and prestige in the social structure of the country. The Turks even lost their "Turkish" character as year after year they became more Egyptian.

British occupation, however, was different from Turkish rule. With the advent of the British, the number of Europeans in Egypt increased. What began as a European population of several hundred at the beginning of the nineteenth century rose to about seventy thousand in 1878 and one hundred twenty thousand in 1897. The overwhelming majority of Europeans remained concentrated in Cairo, Alexandria, and, to some extent, Port Said and Ismailia, where on the whole, Europeans lived aloof, maintaining their distance from Egyptians. Further, in line with Lord Cromer's announced reformist policy to prepare Egyptians for self-government, more and more Egyptians came to occupy administrative positions in government ministries and departments. Once Egyptians came to be accepted as officials, government employment became the ideal for a large segment of the population. Religious education, the most prestigious kind of education throughout most of the nineteenth century, lost ground, and secular education, the main venue to government employment, rose in status. As a result, by the turn of the century, a new Egyptian administrative bourgeoisie had emerged, and this new class of Egyptians came to replace the older Turkish-Egyptian aristocracy as the national elite (Vatikiotis 1980).

Second, as a result of the advent of the British, slave trade, which supplied concubines and was a flourishing business in Egypt throughout the nineteenth century, was officially banned. Yet even before then, the prices of slave girls, especially white slave girls, were so exorbitant that they were beyond the means of most, except the wealthiest. In the slave market, slave girls were classified, in terms of prices and descending order of preference, according to skin color—white slaves were the most in demand and the highest in price, while brown or bronze and black girls were less in demand and much cheaper. Practically all white female slaves in Egypt, imported

from Circassian colonies in Asia Minor, were bought and to be found in the
Mohammad Ali family or in the homes of wealthy Turks. Egyptians preferred
white Circassian girls to the colored concubines, but because of the former's
price most often had to be contented with the second best, that is, brown or
bronze Abyssinian girls. Beyond the Circassian and Abyssinian girls, the bulk
of slaves in Egypt, both female and male, were black slaves imported from
different parts of Africa.

In principle, all slaves were bought for domestic service, but while the
black slaves did the coarse work, the Circassian, and to a lesser extent the
Abyssinian, girls did only light work such as making coffee, preparing and
lighting pipes, and on certain occasions cooking special dishes (Baer 1969).
As Princess Guidan, the wife of Khedive Abbas Helmi II, the local representative in Egypt of the Ottoman porte, wrote in her memoirs:

> Men, especially European men, only hear the word *hareem* and their imagi-
> nation draws up images of beautiful young girls swimming in fountains of
> scented water, or dancing and singing around it. Anyone who has set eyes
> on an Egyptian hareem will find none of this: Concubines in Egypt are girls
> who are cleanly, simply dressed. . . . they are not an instrument for pleasure
> and lust, they are servants and even less than servants, as they are not paid
> for their services, nor can they leave their master's home for another
> (quoted in Yehia, 1983:30 and translated from the Arabic by the author).

Nevertheless, throughout the nineteenth century, concubinage greatly
undermined the status of Egyptian women because according to Islamic
Sharia a man is entitled to the sexual services of his female slaves. Many
Egyptian men availed themselves of these rights, and especially in the cases
when the concubines bore children, men, again in accordance with Islamic
Sharia, would emancipate the concubines first and then marry them (Lane
1978). Under these conditions *hareem* life, by all accounts, was never peace-
ful or harmonious. Wives and concubines resorted to conspiracy and in-
trigue in order to provide for themselves and to attain or maintain the position of master's favorite. In her memoirs, Princess Guidan continues:

> The whole *hareem* is strictly controlled by one of three women: the mas-
> ter's wife, his mother or his favorite concubine. In all three cases, the
> woman in control makes sure that concubines never appear attractive be-
> fore the Master. . . . The wife and mother out of jealousy and fear that he
> marry a concubine, the concubine to preserve her status as his favorite and
> also out of fear that he might marry another concubine (quoted in Yehia
> 1983:31 and translated from the Arabic by the author).

Intensified contact with Europe, both through political pressure and
military action, and a change of attitude among Egyptians brought about the
abolition of slavery. The only problem that remained at the end of the century was the assimilation of manumitted slaves. Some male slaves, not find-

ing work, returned of their own free will to their state of slavery. Female slaves, facing the same problem, became prostitutes (Baer 1969).

By the end of the nineteenth century, because of the abolition of the slave trade and the advent of the British, the Egyptian *hareem* had lost most of its Turkish character, yet Egyptian upper-class women continued to lead a veiled and secluded existence. Qasim Amin, in *The Emancipation of Women,* condemned the lives of *hareem* women in no uncertain terms. He considered the institution of *hareem* a symbol of the utter contempt in which men held women and a means for stripping them of all human attributes and reducing them to one office only, that of satisfying male sexual urges. Still an exclusively urban upper-class institution, *hareem* was, according to Amin, an instrument for the oppression and even imprisonment of women.

> Women have been almost totally effaced by men. They have no place in the universe except the hidden corners of homes—where they live shrouded in darkness and abysmal ignorance—where men use them for their sexual pleasures at will and discard them in the streets, if they so desire. Freedom for men is countered by enslavement for women; education for men is countered by ignorance for women. Men develop their rationality and mental faculties, leaving for women only idiocy and retardation. For men authority and dignity, for women obedience and patience. The brilliance and space of the heavens for men, while for women only darkness and imprisonment. The whole universe is for men, while women occupy only the peripheries and dark corners.
>
> It is a sign of the contempt in which men hold women that they fill their homes with concubines, white and black, and several wives from which they choose to satisfy their lust.
>
> It is a sign of the contempt in which men hold women that they divorce them for no reason.
>
> It is a sign of the contempt in which men hold women that they eat alone, while their wives, sisters, daughters eat only their remains.
>
> It is a sign of the contempt in which men hold women that they assign eunuchs and guards to guard their honor.
>
> It is a sign of the contempt in which men hold women that they pride themselves that their women never leave their homes except for their graves!
>
> It is a sign of the contempt in which men hold women that they consider them untrustworthy.
>
> It is a sign of the contempt in which men hold women that they exclude them from public affairs from work related to this sphere. Women have no say even in their own business affairs; they have no intellect, no taste for the arts, no role in public life, no role in religious life; no feelings of patriotism; no feelings (Amin 1970:38–39; translated by the author).

Further, according to Amin, *hareem* women had the psychology of slaves and prisoners. Deprived of their freedom and of the chance to develop their mental faculties, *hareem* women were emotional beings who used only instinct to distinguish between good and evil. Shy, astute actresses and adept impersonators, they changed their color at will and as the situation required.

Amin's and others' descriptions and condemnations of the lives of upper-class women at the turn of the century are descriptions and condemnations by *proxy* —that is, they are descriptions and condemnations of people speaking for Egyptian women of the upper classes. The voices of these women rarely have been heard. To what extent did Egyptian women identify with Amin's cause? Were *hareem* women aware of oppression? In other words, what was the consciousness of *hareem* women during this age and period?

The following section is an attempt to answer some of these questions. The information upon which it is based was extracted from the private memoirs of an upper-class Egyptian woman who was born into *hareem* life on January 21, 1911. These memoirs, whose author is still alive, are in essence a family history. Although born in 1911, the memoirist incorporates many of the tales and details of daily living recounted to her by her mother, grandmother, and other older female members of her family. These memoirs cover a period of almost seventy-five years, starting in approximately 1880 and ending in 1955. Her father and the patriarch of the family into which she was born was a self-made man. Although descended from a Turkish-Egyptian landed family of great wealth, early in his life he was disinherited. Working to support himself, he graduated from the School of Medicine in 1910 or thereabouts. By working for the Ministry of Health and in private practice, he managed to reach some degree of wealth. As a result of his personal history and his profession, he and his family came to belong to the new Egyptian bourgeoisie that emerged at the turn of the century and replaced the older Turkish-Egyptian aristocracy.

This is not the first attempt to rectify some of the biases on the literature on Egyptian *hareem* women. Marsot (1978) uses oral history to demonstrate that far from leading idle lives, *hareem* women acquired a wide range of managerial skills in the running of their large households. These skills were to stand these women in good stead when they expanded the range of their activities to include an extensive variety of social service work (see Chapter 4). Badran (1977), drawing on the memoirs of Huda Sharawi, the founder of the Egyptian Feminist Union (see chapters 3 and 4), gives extensive treatment to the *hareem* life of Egyptian women at the end of the nineteenth century. Badran finds in the suffering and turmoil of the oppressed, cloistered existence of these women the genesis of feminist consciousness and the discontent that led them two decades later to defy inherited conventions in search of a new and more equitable social order.

My own reading of the situation, which is based on these memoirs and on my own long experience of Egyptian society, differs from both Marsot's and Badran's. I contend that the Egyptian women who came to distinguish themselves either as renowned figures in organized charitable work or as renowned feminists remain exceptions to the rule. The majority of upper-class women, indeed the majority of all classes of Egyptian women, remained unquestioning of the existing social order and were even stauncher upholders of it than men. This social order imposed on women restrictions that limited their lives to marriage and motherhood, but most accepted this as given and part of the natural order of the universe. Their willing compliance probably is accounted for by some of the rewards they accrued from their traditional roles. Even though excluded from the public domain, women derived a degree of power from their marital and maternally related roles. There were aspects of these two roles that were clearly oppressive, but with resilience, resourcefulness, and dignity many women maintained positions of respect and high esteem as daughters, wives, and especially as mothers. As Nadia Youssef (1978) suggests, the power, respect, and socio-psychological rewards that women gained from their traditional status mitigated against the eruption of rebellion and protest and accounted for the initial resistance on the part of Egyptian women to claim their "rights" in the suprafamilial world.

My stance is substantiated by the following analysis, which concentrates on two main themes—Seclusion and Veiling: The Woman's World and the Man's World, and The Gender System, or the Sexual Division of Labour.

Seclusion and Veiling: The Woman's World and the Man's World

The reconstruction of daily activities of the women who are the subject of the memoirs mentioned previously reveals that the dichotomy of a woman's world and a man's world was part and parcel of daily reality. Except for very rare occasions, these women spent the bulk of their days within the confines of their homes.

Generally, households included a large number of residents. An average household included indoor and outdoor servants of both sexes, wives, children, mother, grandmother, aunts, and other poor relatives (Marsot 1978). The young doctor's household at one point in time (1924) included his wife and six children (three boys and three girls); his mother and her five children (three girls and two boys—they were the doctor's half-brothers and half-sisters); a brother from his father's side; two of his wife's sisters; and one female slave, two female servants, and two male servants. All twenty-two people, thirteen women and nine men, were supported by the doctor. The composition of the family household changed as young girls married, divorced women remarried, or young boys graduated and went to work, but the number of people actually supported by the doctor remained close to this number, if a little less or a little more.

The intensity and the duration of the confinement and seclusion of women differed in direct relationship to their age. The grandmother and mother never left their homes except for visits to other homes and other women. Younger unmarried girls, like the author of the memoirs, enjoyed some degree of freedom until puberty (fourteen), when they were veiled and made to quit school and stay at home. Before confinement, the author attended a girls school where she was taught the piano, the rudiments of housekeeping, and the Qoran. When women went out visiting, usually for very pressing reasons such as the death or illness of family members, but sometimes also for social visiting, it was in a private closed carriage, themselves covered by the *yashmak* (headscarf), *borko'* (face veil), and *habara* (cloak) from head to foot. When the doctor transferred his practice from one of the cities of Egypt to another, the family traveled by train but in the private compartments for women.

How then did they spend their days? What did they do during those long days they spent confined to their homes, to the company of each other, and to that of small children and servants? (Male servants and service vendors, such as the water supplier, *el saka,* were not allowed to see the womenfolk.)

All household chores—cleaning, washing of clothes, cooking, the serving of meals, the collection and purification of water in jars (there were no water works at the time)—were performed by the assortment of male and female servants. The responsibility of the lady of the house, the mother of the author of the memoirs, was simply the control of money and the giving of orders to the servants. Throughout the memoirs there is only one incident in which the mother is described as actually "doing something."

> We lived quite affluently. My father's earnings during this period were astronomical. Every coin earned was put in a special pot. The 5 piaster coins were put in the empty boxes of Vichy mineral water. The 10 piaster coins were put in empty boxes of cognac, and the 20 piaster coins were put in the boxes of whiskey. The one pound gold coins were put in the closet. All these boxes were kept under my mother's bed and she daily locked the room after the maids had cleaned it. At the end of each month, all the coins were deposited (by the father, of course) in the bank (p. 9, translation my own).

Even the care of infants and young children was left to the servants. It was common practice at the time to call on the services of breastfeeders. These were women economically in need who had just given birth. Sometimes the breastfeeders were resident female servants who also had just given birth and would breastfeed one or two family babies in addition to their own. Adila, the governess, in teasing the author (after being refused a

10 piaster coin), called attention to this situation: "I am disappointed in you. I suffered in your upbringing tremendously. You kept me awake all night by your crying and incessant demands. All your mother did was carry you in her womb for nine months, but I have carried you ever since" (p. 20, translation my own).

Living in the *hareem* was a gregarious and cherished style of life which the author describes with nostalgia. The lady of every household selected a day of the month as her "reception" day. On that day she received other "lady" friends accompanied by their unmarried daughters. Such reception days were occasions for much frolic and laughter. The homes were meticulously cleaned and decorated, and the finest delicacies were served to the guests, who arrived elegantly and fashionably dressed under their *habara*, *borko*, and *yashmak*. The girls played the piano, sang love songs, and compared notes on the fashions and the latest English and French imports in the market. Older women discussed all topics, "even politics," as they sipped their coffee and scrutinized the "basket of fruits" of young girls as possible brides for their sons or brothers.

Further, the patriarch of the family, a "fun-loving" man, was fond of giving parties for his friends and male relatives, for which he hired the most famous singers of the period to perform at home. Although the women did not attend these parties, they listened from their rooms or watched from behind their laced and curtained windows, their *mashrabiyas*.

A person's daily activities are in essence a function and a reflection of the role that person performs in society. Maybe an understanding of the prevailing gender system, or division of labor, will explain what preoccupied the minds of these women and directed the activities of their daily living.

The Sexual Division of Labor, or the Gender System

The men were the breadwinners; it was their responsibility and duty to work in the public domain, to work outside the home, to provide for their womenfolk and children. Work of any kind for the women of this class and age, particularly work for money, was considered degrading and shameful for the women themselves and for the men who were responsible for their upkeep. A woman of this class sought to earn her own living only if there were no man in her family, be it husband, father, son, or brother, able and willing to support her.

The women's main functions were to be good wives and, more importantly, to procreate; sons were especially valued. To better perform the first function—that is, to be eligible and desirable brides and, later, wives—women were pampered and beautified. A major part of their waking hours was spent in selecting, trying on, and buying clothing from the *dallala,* or "domestic saleswoman." Unable to go to the market, the market came to them. Obesity was one of the most desirable physical attributes and an indication of a life of affluence and ease; thus, women ate special concoctions such as *mifateqa,* an extract of natural butter known to be very rich in calories. The ladies of the house had their bodies massaged by the residing female slaves. Sometimes the women went to women-only public baths where their body hair was removed and they were washed, massaged, and beautified by a *ballana,* or lady's maid.

Despite the separation of the social worlds of men and women, romance was not absent. The memoirs abound in accounts of men openly and unashamedly flaunting their physical attraction to their brides-to-be. These men quoted poetry and love songs, their imaginations triggered by a description provided by their mothers or sisters, or possibly by an accidental and flurried glimpse of their intended brides.

Nevertheless, several incidents in the memoirs indicate the tremendous value placed on the procreation of male children. It was common for a man whose wife gave birth to a baby girl to expect condolences from friends and relatives. The memoirist herself was the doctor's first child. Her birth, as she comments, passed unnoticed. When her brother was born a year later the situation was different. "Do not ask about the happiness of this young father. He celebrated by distributing clothes and food to the poor. When he carried his first son in his arms he felt that he had been compensated for all the years of deprivation and misery" (p. 8, translation my own).

According to one incident, the doctor was called upon to supervise the childbirth of the wife of a pasha. Finding the laboring woman in a critical condition he left her room to ask the pasha whom should be sacrificed—the mother or the baby. The pasha answered:

> Not the son [assuming the newborn would be a boy]. He is the son of my old age. I have been married to my cousin for twenty-five years. I have no children. To free her conscience and to perform her duty to God, my cousin married me to this woman. The baby is indispensable, but there are many women (p. 10, translation my own).

In 1912, the doctor's wife gave birth to twins: a boy and a girl. The mother's milk was not sufficient to breastfeed the two. An Italian breastfeeder was hired. Who of the two infants should the mother hand over to the breastfeeder? Her mother-in-law advised, "Do not give her the boy. . . . Embrace him with your eyes. . . . Give her the girl. . . . Girls are stronger."

The wife followed this advice. One month later the girl died when the breastfeeder rolled onto the baby while both were sleeping and suffocated her to death. When the wife cried for her lost child, the mother-in-law remarked, "It doesn't matter when a girl dies. Thank God the boy has been saved."

A pregnant relative, the mother of four girls, swore that if the child to which she was about to give birth were a girl, the woman would not breast-feed the child and would leave her to die. When the woman's fifth daughter was born, she refused to breastfeed the infant for five days and only gave in after entreaties from relatives and friends.

In another incident, the head of a nearby village, while he was sitting in his garden one morning, was informed by a male slave that his newborn daughter was refusing to breastfeed. He replied, "I hope she never does breastfeed. I have been unhappy ever since she was born. If you bring me news that she has died I will give you a gold coin." The baby girl died and the village leader gave his slave a gold coin.

Under these circumstances, young, attractive, and fecund women, especially mothers of sons, were secure, pampered, and provided for generously. The situation was different for barren women; they were humiliated and lost their claims to status and prestige. If divorced, women often were forced to live as "poor relatives" in the houses of charitable and kind relatives. How did these women cope with this precarious condition where their well-being was dependent on their ability to produce sons?

There is sufficient evidence in the memoirs that some women resorted to superstition and the supernatural in their handling of reality. The ritual of coffee-cup reading—deciphering and interpreting the designs formed by stains of Turkish coffee—formed an integral part of their daily lives. This was a communal and collective activity, and some women were considered more qualified and adept at it than others. Besides the "professional" coffee-cup readers, family members also qualified to perform this function. In deference to her age, the grandmother, Om el-Bek as she was called, was the family's most trusted and respected coffee-cup reader.

> Om el-Bek, as was her habit every morning, sat on her cushion to prepare her sugarless coffee, to smoke and to eat a heavy breakfast. At around ten, surrounded by all the women of the family, she prepared more coffee. As the coffee slowly cooked on the coal stove, saleswomen and other service women came and went. Essence filled the air with a beautiful fragrance. Coffee cups were then passed around to all the women and my grandmother would say, "I do not enjoy drinking my coffee except for this, in your company. Turn over your cups so I can tell your fortunes." Every woman would quickly respond to her request. She would then proceed to tell their fortunes, with an air of seriousness and pending danger. (p. 33, translation my own).

Dreams also were the material of much speculation and discussion in the constant search for clues to the future. In them, women sought guidelines for dealing with the crises of their daily lives, such as giving birth to girls or divorce or, in the worst of all possible circumstances, the first occurrence leading to the second. Here, too, the dreams of some women were considered more worthy of consideration and discussion than the dreams of other women. The dreams of Om el-Bek never failed to come true. Dreams were not always omens of disaster but often predicted future happiness and prosperity.

Zars, or exorcism parties, where women freed their bodies of evil spirits, also were common practice. The *kodia*, or female exorcist, accompanied by a large number of female drummers, identified the *ifreet* (evil spirit) of each woman and encouraged her to dance herself free of the spirit's control.

> The "patients" were hysterical and nervous, but were usually "cured" after the *zar*. Most women were in a bad psychological state . . . A woman was one of the man's possessions, like a piece of furniture in his home. She had no word and no say. A whole year may pass without her ever leaving her home except if someone fell ill or died (p. 5, translation my own).

Yet, with the exception of the foregoing quote, there are no other indications in the memoirs of articulated discontent. If anything, the memoirs reveal that in many instances the women in fact were stronger upholders of customs and traditions and stauncher perpetuators of the status quo than the men were. The older women of the family insisted that the author of the memoirs quit school and wear the veil. In her attempt to persuade the father to this position, the mother argued that her daughter, although only fourteen, looked much older than her age. Tall, robust, and rounded, she looked eighteen or nineteen. The father gave in reluctantly, and the author of the memoirs describes how she enthusiastically and excitedly awaited the seamstress who would take her measurements and sew her *habara*.

On another occasion, the father surprised his wife with tickets to a play presented by the most celebrated comedian of the time, Naguib el Rihany, and his troop. To convince her to attend, he told her that she would sit in the curtained boxes for women and that she could enter the theater after the show started and the lights went out. She answered; "No, the children can go. Impossible that I go myself. What nonsense! I am not used to attending such plays. I never in my life wanted to go to a cinema, or a theatre. I'm happy as I am."

The traditional values of the patriarchal society to which women belonged formed such an integral part of their ethos that obedience was the one character trait nurtured, encouraged, and cherished in girls and wives. Every daughter and wife who is described as respected and loved by the father or husband also is described as "obedient, gentle, and docile." Young girls who exhibited discontent, raised their voices, or even cried silently in opposition to some custom or tradition were reprimanded quickly by their mothers, grandmothers, older sisters, aunts, and even governesses.

If my analysis is correct and if the women here discussed indeed are representative of their class, then it would seem that Egyptian *hareem* women of the end of the nineteenth and the first quarter of the twentieth century did not really have any articulated consciousness of oppression and showed no manifest signs of rejecting or questioning the existing social order. Is it surprising then that the calls for their "emancipation" passed for the most part unheeded by them? The memoirs span a time that witnessed important events in Egyptian history. The author, an articulate, well-read woman, comments on resistance to the British occupation, the 1919 revolution, and even the discovery of the tomb of Tutankhamen in 1922. She makes no reference to the heated debate raised by the publication of Qasim Amin's book, *The Emancipation of Woman,* or Huda Sharawi's dramatic public unveiling in 1923, which was reported by all the newspapers.

• LOWER CLASSES OF URBAN WOMEN •

Hareem women were envied by other classes of women, and their lifestyle was considered an ideal. Yet, poverty and economic need cause the modification of even the most sacred ideals, and the veiling and seclusion of women were a luxury that poorer families could ill afford. Like now, poorer city families lived crowded together in narrow houses constructed from earth mixed with rocks. This intervening variable of space, then as now, undermined the restrictions on the interaction between the sexes in the *wekalat* (commercial quarters) and *harat* (alleys) of urban Egypt. Poverty also meant that lower-class urban women did not depend on their sexual and reproductive functions alone; lower-class women were productive partners whose labor constituted an important part of family income.

Yet, what kind of work was available to lower-class urban women who were unskilled and, for the most part, uneducated? Like Lane's *The Manners and Customs of Modern Egyptians,* the memoirs make only brief and scant reference to the "domestic life of the lower orders." Yet enough is said in both texts to offer us a sketchy image of the kind of work available to poor city women and the less fortunate women of the urban upper classes.

The memoirs mention a piano teacher, a school teacher, and a head mistress. Medical nurses also are mentioned, but these were mostly English nurses. However, in addition to the resident female slaves and servants, there was an assortment of women who offered their services to other women and were hired by the ladies of wealthy families. Some of these were mentioned before—the breastfeeders, the *dallala,* and the *ballana.* There also were lacemakers and dressmakers. These latter worked in their homes and delivered their finished products to their clients at the latter's home. There were, of course, also coffee-cup readers, exorcists, and fortune tellers.

The women's public bath, the Tuesday Bath as it was called, was serviced by women who worked as cleaners, ticketsellers, bookkeepers, and masseuses. Some baths were owned by women. According to some observers, these public baths with their corps of personnel served as a clearinghouse for information and contacts, giving women both the time and setting to conduct the business of social and economic life (Tucker 1983). Thus, to a certain extent, women of this time created a public world of their own.

Yet, how did they fare in male-dominated institutions? How did women fare in the male public domain? Up to the eighteenth century, textiles—the spinning and weaving of wool, cotton, and linen—was the most widespread domestic industry in Egypt. Weaving was a full-time occupation practiced exclusively by men at home or in small shops, but carding, spinning, and bleaching were done entirely by women. Working mostly in their homes, spinners, carders, and bleachers played an important role in textile production. Some women owned their own spinning apparatus and handled all transactions involved in the work, such as buying raw materials and selling final products in the local markets.

At the time of Mohammad Ali, the Ottoman viceroy (*wali*) of Egypt from 1805 to 1848, Egyptian women were drawn for the first time into wage labor. Mohammad Ali, in his quest for Egyptian independence and strength, embarked on an ambitious industrialization program. As a first step, the state took control of all domestic industries. In textile production, a system was followed whereby spinners and weavers bought raw material from the government and sold the finished products back to the government at a fixed price. Gradually, women who had worked autonomously at home were required to work for the government at a fixed salary. The state distributed the raw materials to female spinners through local agents; in Cairo, for example, the sheiks of the various quarters kept registers of the female spinners, distributed flax, collected linen yarn, and paid the spinners' salaries. In the 1820s, Mohammad Ali established spinning and weaving factories. Although the majority of women continued to work at home through the putting-out system, the new factories recruited significant numbers of females, especially young girls, for cotton spinning. Work in these factories was under difficult conditions, but there does not seem to have been any hiring by force. Motivated by the need for money, many women willingly offered their services to the foremen. For the same reason, these women did not encounter much family disapproval even though they worked veiled beside "more-than-half naked men" (Hamman 1980; Tucker 1976).

Strong European opposition to Mohammad Ali's independent policies put an end to his program of industrialization around 1840, and Egypt entered an export-economy phase based on the cultivation and exportation of cotton. Except for a few small-scale industries devoted to processing the export crop (cotton ginning and pressing) and light consumer goods (soap and cigarettes), the industrial sector suffered a severe blow. Despite the abolition of the state-run textile industry, cottage textile industry did not reemerge in its subsistence economy form. Women still spun at home, but the economic importance of home industry had diminished greatly. Women continued to work in factories, and although data on the rate of participation in the late nineteenth and early twentieth centuries are sparse and difficult to obtain, there is evidence that women were employed in the sugar industry stripping cane, in cigarette manufacturing as sorters separating good from bad tobacco, and as folders of cigarette packets. Women also were involved in transporting building material. The largest concentration of female workers remained in the textile industry where they, as well as children, were employed in sorting, processing, and straining cotton. The participation rate in these industries was relatively high, but women were worked seasonally, for very long hours, and were relegated either to tasks that were viewed as traditional female labor (carding and spinning) or to the least skilled operations, such as manual transport and separating activities. By the end of the nineteenth century, Egyptian women's pattern of participation as marginal workers in the labor force already was established (Tucker 1976).

In addition, up to the last quarter of the nineteenth century, the public life of urban Egypt was organized around a number of institutions, the most important of which were the craft guilds, or *tawaif*. Despite serious efforts, the government had been unable to replace them by a new administrative system so that until the 1880s a ramified system of guilds existed in Cairo and in many other towns of Egypt, comprising almost the whole of the indigenous, gainfully employed population (Baer 1969). The available evidence indicates that these guilds practiced an all-male membership and leadership and that women, no matter how economically active, did not play a visible, or at least documented, role in these guilds (Tucker 1976).

Among exclusively female activities, only those of the dancers and prostitutes were organized. In Cairo, these groups formed three separate guilds. Toward the end of Mohammad Ali's reign, these were forbidden. Prior to that time, however, official prostitutes had to pay a professional tax and in cities had to live in separate quarters. These women were under the jurisdiction of the *wali* or *zabit* (district police officer), but as Edward Lane (1978) points out in his *Manners and Customs of Modern Egyptians:*

> He also took cognizance of the conduct of women in general, and when he found a female to have been guilty of a single act of continence he added her name to the list of the public women, and demanded that she pay the tax, unless she preferred, or could afford, to escape the ignominy by giving to him or to his officers a considerable bribe. This course was always pursued and still is by a person who forms the tax of the public women, in the case of unmarried females and generally in the case of the married also;

but the latter are sometimes privately put to death, if they cannot, by bribery or some other artifice, save themselves (p. 124).

These prostitutes, 'almas, and courtesans were perhaps the most visible urban women. Lane calls them "public women." A very important source of information about Egyptian society in the late nineteenth century is the novel *Hadith 'Isa ibn Hisham,* by Muhammed al-Muwailhi. Roger Allen (1974), who a few years ago translated the novel into English, comments in the introduction that

> the almost total lack of female characters [in 'Isa ibn Hisham] is perhaps a silent affirmation of the views of al-Muwailhi's friend Qasim Amin, who had described the position of women in his book *The Liberation of Women,* published in 1899. The only woman who emerges from the background is a dancer prostitute, which serves to show the degradation of the female sex that Qasim Amin talked about (p. 160).

• PEASANT WOMEN •

Beyond *hareem* women and the poorer classes of urban women, what was the lifestyle of the 85 percent of Egyptian women who were peasants? Like *hareem* women, the literature describes the lives of Egyptian peasant women in terms of stereotypes. On the one hand, we have an idealized image of Egyptian peasant women as leading an economically active, unveiled, unfettered egalitarian life. Qasim Amin in particular glorifies the life of peasant women.

> As the socioeconomic status of women rises, their ignorance increases. The lowest level of women in the nation, i.e., peasant women, are the wisest in relation to the conditions in which they live. A peasant woman knows all that a peasant man knows. His consciousness and hers are on the same level. . . .
>
> Education is not what people imagine it to be—stuffing minds with the contents of school curricula, the passing of exams, and then a life of idleness and stagnation. Education is constant work.
>
> To be convinced beyond the shadow of a doubt of the point in question, i.e., the ills of *hareem* life, let the reader compare an educated woman of his class and an uneducated peasant woman. . . . He will find that the former can read, write, speak a foreign language, and play the piano, but he will also find her so ignorant of life's experiences that if left alone she is paralyzed, inept, and totally incapable of fending for herself. The latter, by contrast, although ignorant, has accumulated such a wealth of knowledge through her work and business dealings that if educated would undoubtedly surpass her *hareem* sister in every respect (Amin 1970:98–99, translation my own).

Marsot (1978) also emphasizes the egalitarian existence of peasant women.

> From time immemorial Egypt has been an agricultural society, depending on irrigation. . . . Women as well as men . . . work in the fields. The men perform certain tasks such as plowing, hoeing, and irrigating, while the women perform others like harvesting, winnowing, and livestock raising and all its connected tasks. Both men and women sell and barter in the market place. Thus the rural venture is based on a cooperative venture and division of labor between the sexes (p. 261).

Lane (1978), on the other hand, sees the drudgery of the lives peasant women lead.

> The women of the lower orders seldom pass a life of inactivity. Some of them are even condemned to greater drudgery than the men. Their chief occupations are the preparing of the husband's food, fetching water (which they carry in a large vessel on the head), spinning cotton, linen, or woollen yarn, and making the fuel called "gellah," which is composed of the dung of cattle kneaded with chopped straw, and formed into round flat cakes: these they stick upon the walls or roofs of their houses, or upon the ground, to dry in the sun, and then use for heating their ovens, and for other purposes. They are in a state of much greater subjection to their husbands than is the case among the superior classes. Not always is a poor woman allowed to eat with her husband. When she goes out with him, she generally walks behind him; and if there be anything for either of them to carry, it is usually borne by the wife, unless it be merely a pipe or a stick (pp. 194–196).

Which of these two extreme images comes closest to depicting the lives of Egyptian peasant women at the end of the nineteenth century? A consideration of peasant economy and culture may shed some light on the matter.

Marxist feminist economists today argue that the transition from a subsistence economy to a market economy marks the loss of economic roles and economic independence for peasant women. Peasants in Egypt, as elsewhere in the Muslim Middle East, had been for millennia the backbone of the economy, supporting both the urban and desert civilization. Yet starting with the French occupation in 1789, Egypt seems to have embarked on a new phase in its social, economic, and political history. The nineteenth century, the first "modern" century, witnessed a deep and dramatic transformation of the Egyptian countryside, a transformation that according to economic historians passed through three distinct economic phases (Tucker 1976; Hammam 1980).

The first phase was a predominantly subsistence economy phase, ending in the early 1820s, in which the peasant family fed and maintained itself.

It produced a certain surplus to meet demands of the state and landed officials in the form of taxes, but beyond taxes, the state officials had little interest in the regulation of peasant households, and peasant families maintained a degree of autonomy. During this phase, women indeed led an egalitarian existence, and female labor appears to have been differentiated from male labor primarily along horizontal rather than vertical lines. There is little evidence that points to any difference in the amount of male and female labor, although particular tasks may well have been distributed along gender lines. In an agrarian system of intensive cultivations of irrigated land, long hours of work were required of all workers of the land. The seclusion of women or their absence from the field was a luxury the majority of poor fellahin could ill afford.

The second economic phase was the brief period of statist industrialization from the 1820s to the 1850s. Although a major aspect of Mohammad Ali's long rule was the destruction of large agglomerations of land control, in his search for economic and political leverage he reorganized Egypt as his own private farm. His policies had particularly striking effects on the lower strata of the country, and the fellahin were the "victims" of "modern Egypt." Village structures and households were shaken by the widespread use of corvée labor for public works and agriculture, more or less obligatory work in state factories, and the replacement of old landlords by the impersonal monopoly of the state. As many as four hundred thousand peasants could be called upon by the state to work each year for an average of four months. Further, Mohammad Ali's political ambition dictated the fielding of a large army. After his attempts to raise an army of slave and Sudanese recruits failed, he started a massive program of peasant recruitment.

Corvée labor and military recruitment created a severe labor shortage in the countryside. Agricultural production suffered as the rural village population came to be composed of women, children, the old, and the infirm. Under these conditions, women carried on the demanding labor of irrigation and intensive farming, and women were the principle merchants of agricultural products in village markets. Women even did the work of draft animals, when these were lost to government levies.

Further, like the "lower orders" of urban women, peasant women for the first time in Egyptian history were drawn into the wage labor market. Mohammad Ali's state monopoly of the textile industry led the authorities to forbid all private spinning and weaving. Village women, like their urban counterparts, received set quantities of flax, cotton, or wool and were under the obligation to return the same amount, spun, within a set length of time and then were paid by piecework. The state's permanent incursion into family life shook its internal structure as the state partly replaced for women the authority of their husbands. This brief advent of peasant women into public life and wage labor was to stop after Mohammad Ali's reign and the entry of

Egypt into the export economy phase. A new pattern of landownership was developed whereby large tracts of land were put under the control of large landowners to ensure the rise of plantations able to provide the British textile manufacturers with the needed cotton. As the number of small farm holdings decreased, the number of landless wage laborers increased. Women still worked alongside male family members in the cultivation of family holdings, but men constituted the bulk of the wage labor force. The shortage of male labor was much less acute than during the time of Mohammad Ali; thus women (and children) were hired only for the harvest season. Although more data are needed, it seems that the introduction of large-scale crop agriculture in the Egyptian countryside meant a fundamental change in the relation of women to agriculture. With the erosion of the pattern of family labor, sexual differentiation increased as men entered the agricultural market economy, while women continued with their traditional chores of animal husbandry and food and fuel processing. Further, cottage industry, in which women were active, had been effectively abolished and did not reemerge in its former state. Like their urban sisters, Egyptian peasant women also worked in factories but only as marginal labor, so that by the late nineteenth century Egyptian peasant women had lost most of their economic roles and economic independence.

Did peasant women's active roles in village economies during the nineteenth century give them greater freedom or a higher status than their *hareem* sisters? By all historical accounts, peasant women went unveiled, worked inside and around their homes, in the fields, in the factories, and in the marketplace and sometimes even pleaded their cases in the courts of law. Although there are no written records and no memoirs to help us reconstruct the daily lives of Egyptian peasant women or conjecture about their ethos and level of consciousness, modern anthropological studies reveal that there is no more fundamental or pervasive cultural pattern in Middle Eastern "village culture" than that relating to the value of female modesty (Antoun 1968). Although the pattern of strict seclusion was adhered to more faithfully by upper-class urban families, it remained a strong and explicit norm of behavior among peasants. Hidden veils are sometimes thicker and more restricting than visible ones.

Peasant women's economic contributions, because unremunerated, were then as now "hidden labor," and women's status was determined primarily by their sex. Because women were the repositories of all sexual morality, a strict "modesty code" prescribed and circumscribed every facet of their daily existence. This "modesty code" encompassed all aspects of their lives: coverage of certain parts of the body, behavior in public places, assumptions as to women's character traits, and the requirements of chastity, virginity, and purity. As a result of interpretations and misinterpretations of the Qoran and the Hadiths, as well as the influence of Bedouin culture, women were believed to be religiously inferior beings, ritualistically impure, with limited mental capacities or the capacity for "modest" behavior. As the descendants of Eve, women possessed the powers of witchcraft and were the initiators of all temptation. The virginity, chastity, and purity of womenfolk were connected closely with family honor, of which men were the guardians and beneficiaries. This is manifested in two of the common rituals of village people: circumcision and virginity tests.

The subject of female circumcision in Egypt has been buried in secrecy and taboo for several generations. It only has been brought to the surface recently by feminists, health practitioners, and social scientists. Very few nineteenth century accounts mention or touch on the subject. Even Lane, who gives extensive descriptions of the rites and festivities associated with male circumcision, is completely silent on the topic. However, all modern studies support the view that most women in Egypt are circumcised (Assaad 1980). These studies affirm that at least 75 percent of Egyptian women and girls have undergone circumcision. Only the modernized and privileged few are spared. Hence, it is safe to assume that nineteenth century Egyptian women underwent circumcision between the ages of six to ten—that is, before the girl reached puberty. Female circumcision, in classical Arabic *khetan* (reduction) and in popular usage *tahara*, is of several degrees, which vary from removal of the prepuce of the clitoris only to the full excision of the clitoris. Circumcision of the labia minora and part of the clitoris is the type of operation recommended by Islam and is the commonest in Egypt.

There are no clear records in which we might trace the origin of the practice of female circumcision in Egypt. Its origins are neither well researched nor fully understood. It is difficult to ascertain if it was originally an old African puberty rite that came to Egypt by diffusion or a Pharaonic survival that meshed with Egyptian cultural patterns and then subsequently spread to other parts of Africa. The few scattered references to the practice in Pharaonic Egypt indicate that female circumcision was practiced in ancient Egypt and that it perhaps originated there. Whatever the origin of female circumcision in Egypt, it did not originate in Islamic tradition, as is popularly believed. Both Muslims and Christians have circumcised their daughters since early times, and there is considerable evidence that the practice existed long before Christianity and Islam. It is not practiced in such Muslim countries as Saudi Arabia, Syria, Yemen, Iraq, Tunisia, Iran, and Turkey.

However, the common belief concerning female circumcision is that it is a means of protecting female modesty and chastity, which are highly valued in Islam and clearly prescribed in the Qoran. The physiological state of virginity was and still is considered an unmarried woman's most precious possession, and according to popular belief the practice ensures the attenuation of sexual drives, thus protecting the woman against her oversexed nature, saving her from temptation, suspicion, or disgrace, and preserving her chastity.

Closely related to the strict codes of purity and chastity of village culture is the virginity test, the practice whereby a bridegroom or a midwife on the wedding night, using the finger or a sharp object, breaks the virgin bride's hymen and then publicly, amid jubilation and cheering, displays the resulting blood on a white kerchief or scarf. Should the bride prove not to be a virgin, she is put to death immediately by her bridegroom or by the male members of her own family. If the practice of female circumcision is shrouded in secrecy, the virginity test rites are even more so. Not a single source, old or new, even makes brief reference to the practice.

• SOME INDICATORS OF THE STATUS OF NINETEENTH CENTURY EGYPTIAN WOMEN •

Modern development planners working with statistical data have developed a number of important indicators to measure the status of women in society and to accumulate baseline data necessary for the formulation of effective development policies. The status of women in any society is, of course, a construct that cannot be measured by the level of one or two characteristics, but rather is measured by the levels of a multitude of characteristics. The most commonly used indicators of the status of women are educational level, family formation or marriage patterns, fertility levels, health conditions, economic activity rates, income level, legal status, and political activity rates (Zurayk 1979). Within the confines of available data, the following is an attempt to examine other-than-economic indicators of the status of Egyptian women during and at the end of the nineteenth century.

Educational Level

One of Qasim Amin's main demands for the liberation of women was education. In *The Emancipation of Women,* he devotes a thirty-five-page chapter to the topic in which he insists that the real reason for the corruption and backwardness of the whole of Egyptian society is the "abysmal ignorance" of its women:

> Education is the only means by which a human being rises from a state of corruption to dignity and honor. All natural laws indicate that men and women have the same mental faculties. The situation prevalent in Egypt now is like having a man who owns great wealth in gold which he keeps

locked up in a safe. He is satisfied to open up the safe everyday to admire his gold (p. 40).

Efforts for female education had started during the time of Mohammad Ali, who in 1830 established his famous school of midwifery as part of his ongoing effort to introduce modern secular education in Egypt. This school, attached to the all-male medical school at Abu-Zaabal, consisted of a three-year program whereby women were taught reading and writing as well as midwifery and the treatment of minor diseases. Three years after the school's founding, at the time of the first graduating class, a woman's hospital was built adjacent to the school, and the graduates were appointed to the hospital. Egyptian families at first were reluctant to allow their daughters to attend this school as it was against the prevalent norms of female seclusion as well as being an admission of financial need. To circumvent this resistance, Mohammad Ali imported European slaves expressly for the purpose of providing the school with its first students. Palace slaves remained the only students in this school until Egyptians of the lowest stratum of society, orphans, and soldiers' daughters began to populate the school, first as students and then later after graduation as teachers.

Mohammad Ali's midwifery school remained the only school for women until foreign missionaries established two primary schools for girls in 1846 and 1849 respectively. These schools were followed by other missionary schools and later by four private Egyptian schools. The Egyptian government opened the first primary school for girls in 1873 and the second in 1875. The number of girls in primary schools in 1875 totaled 3,723 in thirty-two schools (two primary government, four private Egyptian, and twenty-six missionary). Also in 1875, three of the foreign schools extended their educational system to the secondary level. Under the British occupation, which began in 1882, few substantial improvements were made in the system of education. Rather, the British closed down many of the government schools and favored only Europeanized missionary schools.

Educational opportunities for young women therefore were limited. Only fortunate girls who obtained admission to government schools or whose parents could afford the high tuition fees of foreign and missionary schools or the fees of private tutors at home received an education.

By 1907, only 4.9 percent of Egyptian men and .55 percent of Egyptian women were literate. So, in effect, 99.5 percent of Egyptian women were illiterate, and even the education of the literate was frivolous and transitory so that as time passed they relapsed into illiteracy. Amin writes of this situation:

> What girls learn now is insufficient. They learn to read and write in Arabic and in a foreign language—some embroidery, sewing and music. What they learn of the sciences is insignificant and serves only to feed their vanity

and conceit. A girl who learns to say "good morning" in a foreign language believes herself to be far above her peers and refuses to engage in any housework. She spends her days telling tales and stories that are of no value except to trigger her imagination to flee into a dream world . . . as she sits watching the smoke of her cigarette. The little items of information that she acquires in adolescence elude her one after the other as she grows older, so that in the end nothing is left (p. 69).

This was the educational level of the urban upper classes. As for the girls of the lower socioeconomic classes and particularly those in the rural areas, the situation was much worse. Lane, in his *Manners and Customs,* notes that female children are very seldom taught to read and write or even to say their prayers. Of the shaikhs of the Kutab he remarks:

> The Schoolmasters in Egypt are mostly persons of very little learning. Few of them are acquainted with any writings except the Kuran and certain prayers, which, as well as the contents of the sacred volume, they are hired to recite on particular occasions. I was lately told of a man who would neither read nor write succeeding to the office of a schoolmaster in my neighbourhood (p. 68).

Marriage Patterns

In the patriarchal, patrilocal, extended families still prevalent in Egypt at the end of the nineteenth century, marriage was a social and family affair, rather than a personal matter. Parents usually arranged the marriages of both their sons and daughters (who had little say in the matter) with considerations of equal rank, class, and even similarity of professions and trade in mind. Although statistics are hard to come by, endogamy and patriarchal cross-cousin marriages were common, although more so in rural Egypt than in Cairo.

In a patriarchal network linked by kinship and consanguinal relationships, the man remained socially and economically secure in his familial network. The husband-wife relationship was never a central focus, and the extreme frugality of marriage further undermined conjugal relationships. Women came and went. Marriage brought in females to produce more family members or to create wealth through inheritance or work, but not to found independent nuclear households with husbands.

The actual marriage arrangements were made between the males of the two families. The giving of a dowry or bride price was indispensable and among the higher classes had to be paid at the time of the signing of the marriage contract, the *katb kitab.* Haggling over bride price was done by elders or men of position who accompanied the two fathers. A girl commanded a higher price if she was beautiful, if she was talented, if she had a sweet disposition, or if she had much property of her own. Also, the dowry of a virgin-bride was much higher than that of a widow or divorced woman.

Although the initial choice and final decision were made by males, the mothers, grandmothers, and old sisters selected and inspected brides-to-be. The grooms usually did not see their brides except on the *dokhla,* or "wedding night," when the marriage was consummated. In some cases, the men saw their intended wives after the *katb kitab.* However, the grooms-to-be received copious descriptions of their betrotheds' physical and other qualifications from their mothers and sisters. Sometimes a *khataba,* or "matchmaker," whose business was to assist men in such cases, was employed.

Youth was of course an important prerequisite for eligibility, and a woman's value decreased in the marriage market as she grew older. As there were no laws setting minimum marriage ages (the Ottoman law specified twelve years for males and nine for females), girls were married at puberty and sometimes betrothed at birth. Lane (1978) notes that

> the Egyptian females arrive at puberty much earlier than the natives of colder climates. Many marry at the age of twelve or thirteen years; and some remarkably precocious girls are married at the age of ten, but such occurrences are not common. Few remain unmarried after sixteen years of age (p. 160).

Much has been written about how polygamy undermined the status of Muslim women. Yet in practice, there were few polygamous marriages in nineteenth century Egypt. Concubines were beyond the means of the majority of Egyptian men, and few men ever managed to obtain more than one wife at a time. Lane makes the shrewd estimate that no more than one out of twenty men had two wives, fickle passion being the most evident and common motive.

It was rather easy divorce, which rampaged unabetted, that destroyed the lives of many Egyptian women, as Lane (1978) understands.

> Hardly a man exists who hasn't divorced once. The facility of divorce has depraving effects upon both sexes. There are many men in this country who in the course of ten years have married as many as twenty, thirty or more wives; and women not far advanced in age who have been wives to a dozen or more men successively. I have heard of men who have been in the habit of marrying a new wife almost every month (p. 183).

More precise estimates are offered by Qasim Amin. From divorce statistics of Cairo during a seventeen-year period (1878–1895), he concluded that three out of every four married women were divorced. The rate was much less for Egypt as a whole because "divorce is much more common in Cairo than in rural areas." From statistics collected from the Sharia courts for the whole of Egypt, he concluded that in 1898, thirty-two thousand out of one hundred twenty thousand marriages ended in divorce (Amin 1970:148–156).

Fertility Levels

Maintaining large households with many children, especially sons, was a value that cut across all social classes, upper and lower, urban and peasant. Consecutive childbearing therefore was the norm for nineteenth century Egyptian women. I have noted already that *hareem* women depended on their sexual and reproductive functions. Childless and "sonless" women were in very precarious conditions, but so also were their peasant sisters. The status of a peasant woman, even though she played a significant role in social production, by and large was determined by her ability to bear sons. A married women was a low-status member of the household until she bore children, especially sons; then she was referred to as "the mother of the children" or "the mother of the first-born son." There was no greater stress or insecurity than what befell a sterile woman in Egyptian peasant society. The aim of marriage was to build a family, and the husband of a sterile woman was fully justified in the eyes of society in taking a second wife or in even divorcing the first. The inevitable result of these values was high fertility levels.

The early age at which women were married did nothing to improve this. As Clot-Bey writes in 1840: "In Egypt, women are nubile at ten or eleven years old. They are often mothers at twelve, grandmothers at twenty-four, great-grandmothers at thirty-six and great-great grandmothers at forty-eight (quoted in Tomiche 1968, p. 174)

Health Conditions

Qasim Amin comments that *hareem* life is detrimental to both the physical and mental health of its women.

> We are all aware that many women have lost their health in this degraded existence and in this life imprisonment, and that they live weak in body and soul. Most of our women are obese and anemic. They are born and immediately afterwards their bodies shrink and shrivel, appearing old in the prime of life. All this because men fear for their honor (p. 57).

Lane (1978) makes the same observation in speaking of the physical attributes of Egyptian women:

> From the age of about fourteen to that of eighteen or twenty, they are generally models of beauty in body and limbs, and in countenance most of them are pleasing and exceedingly lovely. But soon after they have attained their perfect growth, they rapidly decline: the bosom early loses all its beauty, acquiring, from the relaxing nature of the climate, an excessive length and flatness in its forms, even while the face retains its full charms; and though,

in most other respects time does not commonly so soon nor so much de-
form then, at the age of forty it renders many, who in earlier years possessed considerable attractions, absolutely ugly (p. 44).

Amin further comments on the lack of health awareness, accusing
women of "not combing their hair daily" and "bathing only once a week" (p.
57), and of "leaving their children unwashed to wander in the streets, alleys,
writhing around in the dirt like small animals" (p. 65).

Lane (1978) supports this and notes that

> with the exception of those of the wealthier classes, the young children in
> Egypt, though objects of so much solicitude, are generally very dirty, and
> shabbily clad. The stranger here is disgusted by the sight of them, and at
> once condemns the modern Egyptians as a very filthy people, without re-
> quiring any other reason for forming such an opinion of them. It is not
> uncommon to see, in the city in which I am writing, a lady shuffling along
> in her ample tob and habarah of new and rich and glistening silk . . . and by
> her side a little boy or girl, her own child, with a face besmeared with dirt,
> and with clothes appearing as though they had been worn for months.
>
> The children of the poor have got a more neglected appearance. Be-
> sides being scantily clad, or quite naked, they are in general, excessively
> dirty (p. 63).

Income Level

Because census data before 1917 are not sex disaggregated, it is difficult to
arrive at exact figures of the income level of Egyptian women at the end of
the nineteenth century. A related topic, however, is property ownership. Islamic Sharia gives women the right to inherit and bequeath property. It also
guarantees them the right to full control of their wealth. They can buy and
sell property and be involved in trade and commerce without the influence
or permission of husband, father, or other male guardian. Yet, prevailing
conditions and customs at the end of the nineteenth century in Egypt, then
as now, often intervened to deprive women of the advantages of their legal
rights.

Amin maintains that the seclusion and ignorance in which *hareem*
women live greatly undermines their legal property rights. Arguing for the
advantage of the education and involvement of *hareem* women in public
life, he writes:

> If women are rich in their own right—and this is a very rare occurrence—
> having an independent income from property or otherwise, wouldn't edu-
> cation help them to protect their possessions and manage their estates?
>
> Each and every day we see women forced to hand over the manage-
> ment of their wealth to relatives or to strangers. Their agents usually work

for their own benefit rather than for that of their clients, so that in no time the agents are rich and their clients poor!

We see women putting their stamps on accounts, documents and contracts of which contents they are ignorant and even if capable of reading them are incapable of comprehending them. Women are being deprived of their legal rights and wealth by forgery, fraud and embezzlement by their husbands, relatives or agents; would this so easily happen if they were educated? . . .

Isn't it ridiculous that women transact business dealings covered from head to foot or hidden behind a door or curtain. The other partner is told this is the woman who wishes to sell you her house or who delegates you as her agent in marriage for example. The woman says "I have sold" or "I delegate you." The only requirement as to her identity is the testimony of two of her relatives or even strangers. . . . Court cases have revealed the facility of using fraud and forgery in such cases (pp. 46, 83).

Yet, according to Judith Tucker, there also is evidence that women sometimes sued for their rights (Tucker 1979). In samples of five hundred court cases in Cairo each year per decade from 1800 to 1860, she found that women of all classes were principles in about half.

The Sharia inheritance rights of women also were undermined in Egyptian peasant societies. According to the prevalent system of land tenure, all peasant holdings were *miri*—that is, they were fully owned by the state, and the peasants only had usufruct rights. *Miri* land thus was not subject to the Islamic laws of inheritance. Upon the death of the usufruct holder, this right was inherited by sons or male relatives of the deceased, if they were capable of farming the land and paying the taxes; if the deceased had no male survivors, the local officials had the right to invest whomever they wished. Court cases abounded of daughters, wives, and sisters asking for a share of *miri* land as part of their inheritance, but while sometimes they obtained usufruct rights, the judges tended often to ignore or bypass female petitioners.

Legal Status

To this day, the status of women in family law, which is based on Sharia, remains the major problem for Egyptian women, the insurmountable obstacle and "closed door" in the face of all feminist efforts. Traditionally, and up to the beginning of the nineteenth century, religious leaders, and especially Sharia judges, were independent of and highly respected by the rulers. Islamic law ruled the whole country, and the Sharia courts were the only judicial system in existence. However, during the next seventy-five years, traditional legal (and administrative) institutions were relinquished gradually, and legal codes modeled after the French codes were adopted. A new penal code in 1863 was followed by the founding of the mixed tribunals (to protect the commercial interests of foreigners) in 1876 and *abli,* or national, courts (for Egyptians) in 1883. In both courts, commercial, civil, and criminal codes, all based on the Napoleonic Code (with certain sections based on Sharia), were enacted so that by the turn of the century, for all practical purposes, Egypt's juridical system had been modernized along French lines. The juridical competence of Sharia courts was confined to one aspect—personal status, such as marriage, divorce, inheritance, paternity, guardianship, and so on. Personal status or family law was the only aspect of Sharia still formally applied in the country.

Although by the end of the nineteenth century all institutions of Egyptian society were secularized and almost all segments of the population were liberated from the direct control of religion in their daily interactions, the lives of Egyptian women, whose very existence emanated from their roles as wives and mothers, remained closely linked to, circumscribed, and prescribed by religion. Even Qasim Amin never dared suggest doing away with Sharia as a source for personal status and family law (Kamal Ataturk did just that a decade later by adopting the Swiss legal code for Turkish family laws). Rather, Amin proceeded cautiously to describe Islamic practice and jurisprudence, advocating reinterpretation and redefinition but not abandonment.

What was the status of women in the family law promulgated in 1899? The two main sources of Sharia are the Qoran and the Hadiths. Here I present a short summary of the personal status laws enacted by the Sharia courts of the turn of the century, bearing in mind that liberal Islamic *ulema* (learned men) maintain that these laws are based on a pseudo-Islamic and a malinterpretation of the Qoran and Hadiths.

Religious jurists define marriage as "a contract that allows a man to own a woman or several women." The codes maintain that a husband has the right to take unto himself a second, third, and fourth wife, keeping all at the same time, despite any opposition the wife might make. The husband has the right of obedience or *babs.* The word *babs* means "detention" and implies the right of the husband to keep his wife in the marital abode. She is not allowed to leave the home without his permission. A woman who violates this right is defined as disobedient (*nashas*) and therefore not entitled to financial support by the husband. This was developed in 1897 into the right of the husband to force the wife to live with him even against her will. This practice came to be known as the house of obedience (or *bait al-ta'a*). According to this procedure, under certain circumstances, a man can ask the police to arrest his wife and bring her home to live with him.

The husband also has the unilateral right to divorce. He can divorce his wife whenever he wishes, whether she agrees or not, by merely pronouncing the dismissed formula "I divorce you" in the presence of credible witnesses. He does not need any grounds for divorce.

• **CONCLUDING REMARKS** •

For all intents and purposes, it seemed that Egyptian women at the end of the nineteenth century were willing collaborators in the perpetuation of the status quo. The majority were, if anything, more staunch upholders of the existing moral and social order than men were. Whether women did so through conviction or through fear is open to debate. Even though they occupied a clearly subordinate position in the social, political, and legal domains, women were not entirely powerless. They participated in the dominance structures of society and derived power from their fathers, husbands, brothers, and sons. Some men put women on a pedestal and glorified their roles as "mothers and wives." Talaat Harb, in his book *The Education of Women and the Veil,* remarks, "Scarcely a husband exists who does not consult his wife on every minor and important decision in his life" (p. 29).

Willing compliance, at least overtly, was not a characteristic of Egyptian women alone. It is a characteristic of feminine history the world over. The contributions of the social sciences, sociobiology, and folklore have not been able to offer a satisfactory explanation of why women have accepted subjugation (Bullough 1973; Boulding 1976). There is no simple theory for the past subjugation of women, and male/female relations in nineteenth century Egypt were by no means simple relations. They were characterized by all the trickery, deception, and tension characteristic of power relations the world over. Egyptian women were treated at one and the same time as queens and as slaves. As mothers they were glorified, dignified, and respected, but as females they were despised, degraded, and enslaved.

Egyptian women's willing compliance may have been a ploy to help them cope with and accrue benefits from a social order that overpowered them and imposed on them prohibitions that restricted their lives and freedom. Mengin, in *L'Histoire d'Egypte,* observes that "this sex, skillful and ingenious, learns from early infancy ways of evading her inferior status. She studies the men whom she must control; in looking for ways to please, she discovers ways to lead" (Mengin 1823: 311; translation quoted in Tomiche 1968: 78).

PART TWO

The Phases of Egyptian Feminism

Malak Hifni Nassef (1886–1918): "She walked warily in the midst of the varieties of new thoughts and modern opinions." (Photograph used with the gracious permission of Mrs. Seneya Sharawi, granddaughter of Mrs. Huda Sharawi)

CHAPTER TWO

The Intellectual Debate Phase
(1899–World War I)

Historians have offered several theories to explain the origins of feminism and the birth of feminist movements. Changes in family structure due to industrialization have been noted as important reasons for the rise of the first wave of U.S. feminism that started with the Declaration of Sentiments in the Seneca Falls Convention of 1848 and ended with women's acquisition of the right to vote in 1920. Industrialization had displaced two major female functions: home textiles and primary education. Monetization of the economy and the subsequent recruitment of men in wage labor meant that women were deprived of their productive roles in home industries. Further, the formalization of education stripped women of their roles as primary educators. They became social "parasites" and were forced to join paid employment to get the wherewithal to buy what they originally produced at home. Jo Freeman, in *The Politics of Women's Liberation* (1975), explains the rise of this first wave of U.S. feminism through the concept of "structural strain" forwarded by Neil Smelser (1963). Structural strain, "an impairment of relationships among and hence inadequate functioning of the components of action," results from "relative deprivation." Relative deprivation, "a discrepancy between value expectations and value capabilities," functions through comparison to a reference group, which in turn performs the normative function of demystifying myths justifying the status quo and leads to the gradual accumulation of small grievances, aggravation, and then agitation for change. U.S. middle-class women who joined the professions—mainly in underpaid, peripheral jobs—experienced a "sense of deprivation" in comparison to their normative reference group—men. This led women to demand social change.

Variations in demographic patterns also have been considered important causes of feminism. An imbalance in the sex ratio favorable to women in nineteenth century Britain was one of the reasons for pressure to improve the education of girls and to expand employment opportunities for women. The proportion of women in the population therefore has been part of the rise of feminism. It is doubtful, however, that sex ratio alone can explain the rise of feminism in so direct a manner. In the United States, suffrage rights were not always granted in the states where the sex ratio was favorable to women. In addition, expansion of economic opportunities occurred in regions where there were surplus women and regions where they were in demand. Further, the first wave of U.S. feminism was a middle-class movement, a class in which there was no sex ratio imbalance (Evans 1977). The spread of contraceptives, the resultant drop in birth rate, and subsequent increase of women, particularly married women, in the labor force also have been cited as one of the causes for the rise of feminism. Yet, the relationship between feminism and the size of the family is a highly complex one, and women's attitudes to the size of their family may be a consequence of feminist ideas as well as a cause of them (Banks 1981).

Changes in class structure also have been advanced as explanations for the rise of feminism. The rise of the middle class, the occupational and professional class in nineteenth century Europe, changed the structure and values of society. The aristocracy lost ground as work, ability, and achievement, rather than heredity and titles, became the status symbols. Virtue came to be redefined as work, and the values of accomplishment replaced the leisure values of the noblesse oblige. The work ethic and the professionalization of teaching, nursing, business, and law drove women out of the home and into public life (Evans 1977).

Finally, contradictions between the ideology of women's role and their actual position in society have been suggested as causes for the rise of feminism. Juliet Mitchell (1971), for example, cites the contradictions between women's position in the family and their position in the workplace and the contradictions between the ideology of sexual freedom and women's actual sexual exploitation as the impetus for the demands for change in the status of contemporary Western women.

Yet, Egyptian feminism in its first phase was an urban upper-class movement initiated by urban upper-class men and directed at urban upper-class women. The movement's eruption was not the result of industrialization, demographic patterns, or the contradictions between ideology and practice, but rather was due to political factors—namely, the British occupation of Egypt in 1882.

Colonialism is a conflict-ridden situation, especially when colonizers and colonized are of different cultures. If colonizers and colonized share similar material, cultural, and religious backgrounds, then accommodation leads to assimilation, integration, and eventual homogeneity. As part of the Ottoman Empire, Egyptians felt no resentment but rather a deep allegiance to the Ottoman sultan in Constantinople. Sultan Abdul Hamid was not only sultan but also caliph of all Muslims, and thus Egyptian feelings of allegiance were motivated by religious rather than political factors (Abdel Kader 1973). The British occupation was the first real direct contact with an alien foreign power. Strong feelings of rejection of foreign rule soon crystallized into a serious and sustained effort to search for the road to liberation.

Egyptian feminism in its first phase was linked closely with the Islamic Reform Movement. Both were expressions of the same profound problem and an outcome of an agonized soul-searching among nationalists to find solutions for the plight of their country, which was colonized and dominated by an alien, Christian power. The overwhelming presence of Europe in the form of the British occupation led nationalists to a reconsideration of their country's position and identity in relation to the West. National independence seemed to supply the answer to Western domination. Yet, there was little agreement as to how exactly to achieve this aim.

Throughout the nineteenth century, the role of religion in society had been the most critical and pressing question occupying the minds of Egyptian intellectuals. For leaders of the Islamic Reform Movement such as Rifai Rafi' el-Tahtawi, Gamal al-Din al-Afghani, Muhammad Abdu, and their followers, the question was what should the role of Islam be if Egypt were to become a modern sovereign state and its society transformed into a dynamic political community. Should Islam and Islamic traditions continue to rule supreme as they had done for centuries, or should the secularization of society and politics be complete? The British occupation and the famous attacks upon Islam as a religious and social system by Lord Cromer and others intensified the debate among Egyptian intellectuals and leaders on the role of Islam in the modern world. By 1895, the major divisions among Egyptian nationalists surfaced in the press as they debated issues such as civic liberty, representative governments, the separation of state from religion, and relationships with the khedive, the Ottoman porte, and the British.

The British, whatever their other faults and whatever their motives, inadvertently gave Egypt the freest press it had ever had. Until 1882, the embryonic Egyptian press was crude, experimental, and didactic. Moreover, it was official, begun and largely financed by rulers, who raised a heavy hand against journalists who stepped out of line. Only during the British occupation and until 1914 did the Egyptian press come of age and concern itself with the public debate of social, economic, and political issues.

In terms of sheer numbers, the progress of the Egyptian press during the British occupation was truly spectacular. When Lord Cromer arrived in Egypt in 1882, there were only a handful of newspapers. During the period 1892–1900 alone, about one hundred fifty new newspapers and periodicals were launched, which were as many as during the entire previous sixty-three years. Many of these were short-lived, but the activity of the Egyptian press was no less astounding for that. By 1911, there were eighty-four daily newspapers, twenty-nine literary reviews, three Arabic legal periodicals, five medical journals, fourteen religious newspapers, four Arabic historical reviews, two humorous magazines and . . . three women's journals (Ahmed 1960). The phenomenal growth of the Egyptian press, surpassing the press in all other Middle Eastern countries, had significant implications for the rapid dissemination of information in all areas and satisfied the intellectuals' hunger for world news. In fact, between 1890 to 1900, literate Egyptians as a matter of course did not read books; they read newspapers, magazines, and periodicals (Vatikiotis 1980). Also, most of the major books of the time were published first as articles in newspapers and then only later in book form.

By the end of the nineteenth century, the Egyptian press had become the vanguard of a vast intellectual movement that touched all aspects of Egyptian culture. It was in the press that the major nationalist ideas were presented, and especially after 1900, the press reflected the conflict between conservative and modernist tendencies in social thought and life.

A characteristic of Egyptian press and politics at the time was that newspapers were established, and around them political parties were founded. In several cases, a writer would establish a paper, and slowly, as other like-minded people were attracted to it, they formed a party and became active on the political scene (Rugh 1979:53). Muslim conservatives gathered around Shaikh Ali Yusif, editor of *Al-Muayyid* and later president of Hizb el-Islah party. The policy of the newspaper was to propagate Islamic revival as the only road to salvation and independence, and the program of the party was anti-British, pro-Ottoman, pro-khedive, and pan-Islamic in orientation.

Extreme nationalists found a leader in Mustafa Kamel (1874–1908), the editor of *Al-Liwa* newspaper and the founder of Al-Hizb al-Watani. The central plank of Mustafa Kamel's party was the total and unqualified withdrawal of all British troops and government officials from Egypt. For Mustafa Kamel, national independence was the demand overriding all other issues, and his constant hammering on this point was the main reason for his party's tremendous popularity. Kamel's nationalism perhaps could be best described as "counternationalism"—nationalism that is a reaction against foreign domination rather than a concern with the political and social structure of society itself (Phillip 1978). Introduction of change along Western lines seemed to him like foreign designs to corrupt Egyptian society and shatter its moral fabric. In line with his party's and his newspaper's policies of rejecting Western culture and society, he aligned himself with the Muslim khedive and Ottoman sultan.

The spokesman of secular liberalists was Ahmad Lutfi al-Sayyid (1872–1963), editor in chief of *Al-Jarida* and founder of the Umma party. A staunch exponent of the concept of nationhood, he made a clearcut break with the Islamic framework. The society he wanted to reform was no more the Islamic community, but the Egyptian nation that, according to him, had to become independent of both the Ottoman Empire and the British. Yet, it was his belief that a nation can exist independently only if all its members participated in it. Freedom of the individual, constitutionalism, and education were essential prerequisites to prepare the Egyptian nation for independence, an independence he believed should come gradually. In the meantime, he considered the European and particularly the British political system an ideal to be followed and taken as a guide for the reform of Egyptian society.

Although affectionately dubbed "the professor of the age," al-Sayyid was identified as pro-Western and pro-British, and for this reason his party and his newspaper were never too popular with the Egyptian nationalists or the Egyptian populace. To appreciate fully his courage, one must bear in mind that he wrote at a time when pan-Islamic, in effect pro-Ottoman, sentiments still moved the masses against the British in Egypt and when any suggestions of compromise or accommodation with European ways, let alone British rule, amounted to treason (Vatikiotis 1980). To urge Egyptians to deviate from their traditions by adopting alien, non-Islamic ideas essential to Egypt's progress and reform because they were superior was plainly revolutionary. However, in his enthusiasm and elitism he underestimated the political power inherent in the Egyptians' instinctive adherence to their Islamic heritage.

Between the two extremes of Muslim conservatives and secular liberalists, there was a movement of thought that was perhaps the most important of all. This movement took definite shape under the leadership of Shaikh Muhammad Abdu (1849–1905). Abdu was not the forerunner of the traditionalism of Shaikh Ali Yusif, the extreme nationalism of Mustafa Kamel, or the secular liberalism of Lutfi al-Sayyid. Abdu's ideas were that Egypt should become part of the modern world without a violent break with its own past and without destroying the moral basis of its community—the Islamic religion and Islamic traditions. As mufti of Egypt from 1899 until his death in 1905, Abdu made a tremendous effort to reinterpret Islam and Islamic traditions in a manner compatible with modern times.

One of the prominent and essential ideas in the writings of Abdu was the necessity for the training and education of girls, no less than of boys, and the necessity for reform in the social conditions and customs affecting the lives of Muslim women. Abdu maintained that in nothing does Islam show its fitness to be considered a modern world religion than in the high position of honor it accords to women. According to its teachings, women and men are equal in all essential aspects. Polygamy, although permitted in the Qoran, was a response to existing social conditions and was given with the greatest possible reluctance. Permission was accompanied further by the provision that a man could marry more than one wife only if he could care for all and give to each her rights with impartiality and justice. The practical impossibility of doing so, Abdu maintained, indicated that the Divine Law, in its intent, contemplated monogamy as the original and ideal state of marriage. The evils of polygamy and of easy and frequent divorce were an outcome of ignoring the original intent of the Qoran, in this and other aspects. It therefore was necessary that all unfavorable conditions affecting the lives of women be corrected, so that Muslim women might be raised to the level originally contemplated in the spirit of the religion of Islam.

These and other ideals were touched upon by Abdu and his followers, but it remained for Qasim Amin to make this field of reform particularly his own and to arouse Egyptian public opinion by his writings to an unprecedented extent. In the uproar caused by the publication of his book *The Emancipation of Women* in 1899, every shade of opinion was represented, and nationalists far from agreed on the topic. Yet, one thing was evident—the issue was an important one that touched on the life of everyone.

• QASIM AMIN •

Amin was born in Alexandria in December 1863. At least this is the date mentioned in most books. Yet, there is a discrepancy between this date and the relatively young age at which he attained his diplomas and also the high positions he later came to hold (Bahaa el-Din 1970). His father, Muhammed Bey Amin, was from an aristocratic Turkish family, at a time when these aristocratic Turkish families constituted the high-powered elite in all the communities that came under the rule of the Ottoman Empire. Typically, Muhammed Bey Amin moved all over the empire, occupying one position after the other, until he finally settled in Upper Egypt where he made the acquaintance of a respectable middle-class Egyptian family, admired one of its daughters, and married her. His family connections, as was the custom at the time, enabled him to secure the ownership of a large tract of land in the Northern Delta, which is now the govenorate of Kafr el-Shaikh. Qasim Amin was eight when this happened. The family then moved to live in Alexandria, the metropolis closest to the family's estate, where Qasim Amin attended the primary school of Rass el-Teen. The family then moved to Cairo to live in al-Hilmiya, one of the most prestigious residential areas at the time, where Amin attended the Preparatory School (al-Khidiwiya, al-Thanawiya later). Finally, he joined the School of Law and graduated in 1881 at the top of his class and, according to the birth date previously mentioned, at only eighteen years old.

Upon graduation, he worked for a while as an intern in the law office of Mostafa Fahmy, who later became prime minister of Egypt for eighteen continuous years and whose daughter Safia married the leader of the 1919 Egyptian Revolution, Saad Zaghlul. During this period Amin witnessed the Orabi Revolt and the subsequent occupation of Egypt by the British and also made the acquaintance of people like al-Afghani, Abdu, and Abdullah al-Nadim. In 1882, Amin was sent to France on scholarship where he attended the Law School of Montpelier. In Paris, he continued to follow the news of Egypt and of the strong nationalist movement fomenting there. In 1884, he joined both Muhammad Abdu and Gamal al-Din al-Afghani, who were in exile, and worked closely with them on their short-lived pan-Islamic newspaper, *Al-Urwa al-Wothka*. Amin also became exposed to the intellectual climate in Paris, which was brewing with the revolutionary ideas of the French Revolution and the revolutions of 1830, 1848, and 1870. He read Nietzsche, Charles Darwin, and Karl Marx.

Amin started to make comparisons between Egypt, his beloved country, and Europe. In his memoirs, he writes:

> When one compares Cairo to other big cities such as London, Paris, it really appears to be in a very sad state. It is like putting a beggar in rags, next to a bride at her best. In reality, Egypt is a very poor country; half its people— the peasants—live on the brink of starvation (quoted in Bahaa el-Din 1970: 13).

He also underwent an experience common to all Arab young men who journeyed to Europe: He became acquainted with European women. References mention a French girl, Slava, with whom he probably had a love affair. Although Amin himself does not mention her in any of his writings, by all other accounts it seems that he did not take his involvement with her lightly. From his writings on love one gathers that he was deeply attracted to her. Whether or not this affair was real, however, there is little doubt that Amin was especially attracted by the position of women in European societies. He was moved by the nature of male/female relations and the deep love between husband and wife. In his book he wrote some of the most moving passages on the subject (Bahaa el-Din 1970; Haikal 1929).

Nevertheless, it is important to bear in mind that the status of European women was not too different from that of their Egyptian sisters. Women in Europe did not have the right to vote, to stand for election, to hold public office (however, in certain countries women were monarchs), or, in many parts of Central and Eastern Europe, to join political organizations or attend political meetings. Legal restrictions prevented women from holding property, transferring a woman's inherited wealth to her husband upon marriage. Economic and social sanctions prevented women from engaging in trade, running a business, joining in the professions, opening a bank account or obtaining credit in their own names and thus ensured that they did not become economically independent. Women were further denied their basic rights to civil and criminal law. In most countries, they were not "legal persons," that is, they could not enter into contracts and were considered minors or children in the eyes of the law. Until women married they were under the power of their fathers and required the latter's permission to work, marry, change residence, and so on. This continued, if women were unmarried, into their thirties and forties. After marriage these powers passed to the husband. Divorce was relatively easy for husbands and almost impossible for wives. In cases of sexual deviances, the law punished women but allowed men to avoid all responsibility. In law cases of all kinds, women were treated as inferior witnesses whose word counted for less than that of men. There also was discrimination in education (Evans 1977:13–38).

These conditions remained more or less unchanged throughout the nineteenth century. Yet, liberal thought had transformed attitudes and laid the intellectual underpinnings for change. Nineteenth century Europe was brewing with feminist movements. John Stuart Mill's essay, *The Subjection of Women,* published in 1869, had been the feminist bible. In the same year that it was first published in England, the United States, Australia, and New Zealand, it also appeared in translation in France, Germany, Sweden, and Denmark. In 1870, Mill's work appeared in Polish and Italian and also was being discussed excitedly by female students in St. Petersburg. By 1883, the Swedish translation was forming the center of discussion of a group of women in Helsinki who founded the feminist women's movement as soon as they finished reading the book. From all over Europe there were impressive testimonies to the immediate and profound impact of Mill's book; its appearance coincided with the foundation of feminist movements not only in Finland but also in France and Germany and very possibly in other countries as well.

There is no historical evidence that Qasim Amin read John Stuart Mill's book. The book never was translated into Arabic, but it was available in French, a language with which Amin was thoroughly familiar. Yet, as we will see later, his arguments and his call for the emancipation of women are very similar to John Stuart Mill's. Amin was a liberal thinker who had internalized and deeply believed in the liberal intellectual traditions of the Europe of his age.

Despite his fascination with European women and male/female relations in the West, Amin did not intend early in his career to make the emancipation of Egyptian women his life's cause. Upon returning to Egypt in 1885, he became a judge in the Court of Appeals of the National Tribunals, consecrating his efforts to being a just and fair judge and going to pains to interpret the laws in a progressive and merciful way (El-Sakakiny 1965). Yet he maintained close ties with the intellectual leaders of his time and attended weekly the "salon" of Nazli Fadl, daughter of Mustafa Fadl, frequented by people like Muhammad Abdu, Saad Zaghlul, Ibrahim Bey al-Hilbawi, Ali Yusif, and others.

In 1893, Qasim Amin read some disparaging remarks by a French writer, Le Duc d'Harcourt, about Egyptian family life and especially the use of the veil (Adams 1933; El-Sakakini 1965). Le Duc d'Harcourt had been on a winter visit to Egypt during which he traveled to different regions seeking to enjoy Egypt's warm sunny weather and natural beauty. Upon returning to his country, however, he published a book in French, *L'Egypte et les Egyptiens,* in which he attacked the morality of Egyptians and described their lives in very macabre terms. He observed the lives of Egyptian *hareem* women and found in their seclusion the manifestation and the reasons for the backwardness of Egyptian society, which he contended was immersed in superstition and depravity. More important, he attributed all this to Islam and repeated the familiar accusation that Islam as a religion was incompatible with progress and civilization and that Muslims were a backward people because of their deep entanglement with religion and their unconsciousness of the precepts and concepts of the modern world.

Le Duc d'Harcourt was not the first or only European writer to attack the inferior position of women in the East or to attribute this to Islam. Throughout the nineteenth century, many European scholars, travelers, and administrators had commented on the one aspect of Muslim societies that most visibly and flagrantly differed from Western societies: the undisguised supremacy of men over women and the explicit and unequivocal manner in which women were regarded and treated as inferior. Westerners, considering their own culture as the epitome of civilization and progress, attributed the "degenerateness," "despotism," "vice," and general "backwardness" of the Muslim world to its low evaluation of women (Ahmed 1960:46; Ahmed 1984:116). French and British writers repeatedly returned to this theme in their articles and books. To Volney, Muslim family life looked like "a perpetual scene of tumult and contention." To Stanley Lane-Poole, "The degradation of women in the East" looked like "a canker that begins its destructive work even in childhood, and has eaten into the whole system of Islam." Lord Cromer doubted whether Egyptian women "will exercise a healthy and elevating influence over men." In comparing Muslim and Christian women Lord Cromer (1908) comments:

> The religiosity of Christian women in Europe is generally deeper than that of men. . . . On the other hand, we find that the attitudes of Muslim women to their religion are milder than those of men. This is not surprising as the roots of the difference in attitude between Christian and Muslim women lies in the intrinsic differences between Christianity and Islam. Islam gives men a status far above that of women. It is therefore natural that Muslim women are not too enthusiastic about their religion (quoted in Yehia 1983: 89).

Upon reading d'Harcourt's book, Qasim Amin was so incensed that in

1894 he wrote a reply in French, under the title of *Les Egyptiens: Réponse à M le Duc d'Harcourt,* in which he defended the use of the veil as a safeguard of society and severely criticized the promiscuity and laxity of European social life. From that time, he began to study European works on the relation of women to society and as a result became convinced that there was some truth in d'Harcourt's allegations. As Amin comments in his memoirs (which were published posthumously):

> I saw such cruelty in d'Harcourt's book that all my hopes were crushed. Slowly, slowly, I calmed down, and thought about what he said and conclusions he had reached. I put aside my double-identity as a Muslim and Egyptian and analysed the situation without emotion or prejudice, guided only by my search for the truth (quoted in el-Sakakiny 1965: 32).

Five years later, Qasim Amin published his first book, *The Emancipation of Women,* in which he argued that the status of Egyptian women was the single most important aspect of Egyptian society in need of reform and that the salvation of the country and its emancipation were contingent upon the emancipation of its women. The reaction to his book was immediate; his ideas elicited tremendous opposition from every conservative quarter: the khedive, the Muslim conservatives, and the extreme nationalists. Khedive Abbas Helmi II, with his usual eye on popularity, made it known that he was dissatisfied; Qasim Amin, who already held a high position in the legal service and enjoyed much professional esteem, was not to be received in the palace on ceremonial occasions (Adams 1933). Shaikh Ali Yusif, in whose newspaper *Al-Muayyid* Amin's book had first appeared as a series of articles, found himself forced to publish an apology and disclaim any connection with Amin (Yehia 1983). Mustafa Kamel, in his ardent, vitriolic, outspoken nationalism, attacked Amin's ideas and proclaimed that they shook the foundations of Muslim society. Amin's book produced a greater reaction than any other book published at the time. No less than thirty books and pamphlets were written to refute his ideas or attack him personally (Phillip 1978).

By coming to perceive the status of women as the most important aspect of Egyptian (and Muslim) society in need of reform, Amin was to some extent accepting and endorsing the diagnosis arrived at by Western men. Nevertheless, it would be erroneous to conclude that in endorsing the ideas of Westerners, Amin was uncritically echoing those ideas. Western criticism of the Muslim may have been instigated by an explicit or insidious desire to denigrate it, but the reality of women's oppression in the Muslim world and in Egypt indeed was ugly and unacceptable. By all accounts, Amin was not a shallow or rash man, but of a retiring and contemplative nature. His conclusions were developed from a comprehensive and vigorous analysis of Egyptian society and a perfectly lucid sense of the various oppressions operating within it. As he states in the first page of the first edition of his book:

This truth I publish today has occupied my mind for a long time. I've been turning it around, examining it and analysing it, until I became certain it was free of confusion and faults. Since then it has taken up much of my thinking, constantly recurring to me, reminding me of its advantages and the need for it, until I became convinced that there was no alternative but to bring out publicly in the open (quoted in Haikal 1929: 154).

Further, by modern standards, what Qasim Amin demanded was very conservative. His explicit ideas about women were very mild. The book in fact began with an analysis of the degraded status of women in Muslim society, a degraded status he attributed to a misinterpretation of Islam rather than to Islam itself. The Prophet, he claimed, gave women a higher status than they had in pre-Islamic times, but it was not long before women's rights were curtailed and extraneous restrictions were imposed on them. Amin argued that women must play a fuller part in society, and for that, they have to be educated. Yet, he never suggested equal education for men and women, but only equal opportunity for boys and girls at the primary stage. He refuted the idea current at the time that chastity (*iffah*) would be endangered by education. "That some people use education for unworthy ends does not justify their being deprived of it."

He dealt with the question of the veil from a religious and social point of view. He defended its existence, recognizing it as a basis for morality, and wanted it retained, but not in its current form. The conditions of veiling were laid down in the Muslim legal code and must be respected. He quoted the passages in the Qoran that laid down the law on the subject and interpreted them to mean that veiling should not be in a form that prevented women from carrying out their duties as wives or upholding their rights in courts. Seclusion was not necessary because the verses of the Qoran that spoke of it refer only to the wives of Muhammad, not to women in general. In fact, according to the traditions of the Prophet, Muslim women were allowed to mix with strangers so long as near relations were present.

In regard to polygamy, he repeated some of Muhammad Abdu's ideas. Amin held that the original Islamic conception had not been observed by later practice. The idea of marriage held by jurists, he maintained, was crude and departed from the original ideas of the Qoran and the practice of Muhammad. Marriage, according to jurists, was a contract that gave a man the possession of a woman's sexual organ. In the eyes of God, however, marriage was something different. "He hath created wives for you of your own species, that ye may dwell with them, and hath put love and tenderness between you," said the Qoran; and woman had rights no less than man, for, to quote the Qoran again, "it is for the woman to act as they [the men] act by them, in all fairness." Jurists had misinterpreted the Muslim idea of marriage, and that led to polygamy. There were cases in which polygamy was admissible—when a wife was incurably ill or barren—but otherwise, polygamy was only a legal excuse for satisfying animal passions. Moreover, there was another condition to be fulfilled, one that could be done only with difficulty—justice between the wives; "and if ye fear that ye shall not act equitably, then one only."

On the question of divorce, Amin followed the same method of going back behind the letter of law to its sources in the Qoran and the practice of Muhammad and his immediate companions. Amin asserted that divorce was not to be resorted to except in unavoidable circumstances and, recalling the traditions of the early caliphs, quoted Caliph Ali's pronouncement that "it shakes God's own throne." The Qoran, Amin argued, while admitting repudiation, restricted divorce to very special circumstances. Amin put forward proposals to limit divorce—husband and wife, with the judge as mediator, should be given ample opportunity to arrive at a reconciliation. At the same time, however, Amin maintained that wives should have the right to ask for release from husbands in special circumstances.

It was not Amin's demands for women that shook Egyptian society. It was his astute and piercing analysis of prevailing morality. His criticisms of the degeneration and corruption of male/female relationships and of the meanings of love, marriage, motherhood, and fatherhood insulted and hurt both men and women (Bahaa el-Din 1970). He saw the seclusion of women as an indication of the utter corruption and backwardness of society. Because education and freedom were the sources of every good for man, the basis of his civilization and his moral perfection, depriving women of either was, Amin argued, tantamount to barbarism. In effect, Amin was saying that the standards of behavior, customs, and traditions of contemporary Muslim society were immoral. Western civilization was, by contrast, moral and worthy of emulation.

Amin's second book, *The New Woman,* published in 1901, was written as a reply to his critics and therefore was much more rigorous and spirited than the first. Here Amin indulged in a wider intellectual argument for the emancipation of women, and, in fact, for the advantages of Westernization in general. He accused the teachers of Islam of woolly thinking and presented a view of Islamic civilization that shocked conservatives and intelligentsia. He reminded his audience that the major accomplishment of Islam was to provide a simple but forceful faith that brought warlike desert tribes together and welded them into the nucleus of a great empire. He bluntly asserted that Islamic civilization had declined, and that in its present form as a social order, it was incompatible with the modern world. The oppressive rigidity of jurists regarding Muslim behavior and their blind stagnation and bigotry made Islam an obstacle to the benefits of modern civilization. To treat Europe as an implacable enemy of Islam was to perpetuate ignorance because there was so much that was beneficial to learn from the West. It was inviting disaster to hold onto a petrified past; modern mechanical civilization was a unifying force in the world, and Egypt could not stay outside the procession. Yet, Europe was in a position to teach the East not only about European industries and arts but also about the art that was the key to all others—civic virtues, an art almost unknown in the East at the time.

Qasim Amin's ideas thus led him far beyond the problems of women, and this no doubt explains the variety and force of the objections raised by his adversaries. For what Amin was advocating was nothing less than a social and intellectual revolution. In all stages of the verbal dual that ensued, the point at issue—the position of women—was relegated to a secondary position, and the Islamic and western outlooks on life as a whole were pitted against each other. Those who ostensibly defended the status quo in reality were attacking Western standards of morality and the dangers of copying them. The violence of reaction was rather an expression of aversion to the idea of Westernization implicit and sometimes explicit in Amin's approaches and themes, rather than to the emancipation of women as such.

Amin did not live long. He died in 1908 at the age of forty-five. The tide of disapproval his books had set in motion was still overwhelmingly against him when he died. Amin was a thinker rather than a doer. He did not have the leadership qualities of Saad Zaghlul, the charismatic leader of the 1919 revolution, for instance. Yet, some of Amin's views on religious and social reform were visionary, and he could devote himself with enthusiasm and persistence to the cause in which his sympathy was invested. His great contribution to Egyptian women was that he put the issue of their "emancipation" on the agenda of public debate.

• THE ISSUE OF WOMEN IN THE MIDST OF INTELLECTUAL TURMOIL •

As mentioned earlier, Amin's ideas led him far beyond the problems of women. In advocating the emancipation of women he was offering his own solution to the plight of Egypt and the British occupation. The emancipation of women was not an end in itself, but a means to the independence of the country. Amin's opponents were fully aware of this, and as the issue became a part of political discourse, their rebuttals very often were dictated by their own political stances and their ideas about the road to independence.

One of the most prominent opponents to Qasim Amin and the emancipation of women was Mustafa Kamel, the leader of those nationalists whose aim was the immediate evacuation of Egypt by the British. Born in Cairo, he was the son of an engineer. Mustafa studied law and visited France several times. As a student, he already had gained a reputation as a militant nationalist by leading student demonstrations against the British and pro-British newspapers. It was his intention to mobilize the support of France and to generate enough internal pressure to force Britain out of Egypt. When

France concluded with England the Entente Cordial in 1904, he turned away from Europe and searched for greater solidarity of the whole East. He became pro-Ottoman and pan-Islamic in his approach. In 1907, Mustafa Kamel founded his own nationalist party, Al-Hizb al-Watani.

In line with their opposition to Western innovations (*bida'*) of any kind, Kamel and his party took a conservative stand on the issue of women's emancipation and discarding the veil. Kamel's preoccupation with national independence and international politics made him regard this issue as secondary in importance. As long as his goal was not obtained, he eyed social change suspiciously as a means to divide society and to weaken its moral fiber. He viewed the emancipation of women in particular as an unpatriotic development that aimed to undermine Egyptian national identity. Egyptian women thus lost in him a powerful supporter when throughout 1901, at the height of his power as a nationalist leader, Kamel turned all his energy to combatting the ideas of Qasim Amin and later kept returning to it with his usual fire and eloquence (Phillip 1975; Crabbs 1984).

It is difficult to determine whether Mustafa Kamel's attitude to the issue was guided by his own loyalty to traditional Islam or by the politician's instinct not to antagonize popular religious feelings. Despite his eloquence and the tremendous efforts he exerted both nationally and internationally to plead the Egyptian cause, what he said, in public and in private, did not always coincide with what he really believed (Crabbs 1984; Phillip 1978). His attitude on the issue of women may have been no more than politically expedient because to espouse Amin's ideas at the time was to risk losing one's popularity with the masses. Further, Kamel tried to cooperate with Khedive Abbas Helmi and knew that the latter had a strong dislike of Amin.

Another of the leaders of the opposition to Qasim Amin's feminist ideas was Talaat Harb (1867–1941). A Cairene, his father was an employee of the railway company. Harb studied law, and after a short spell in juridical administration, he worked in various companies, mainly in finance. He began to write on a variety of issues concerning Islam and the Egyptian nation. His major achievement was the founding of Bank Misr in 1920. This bank became the most important means for creating an indigenous Egyptian industry and increasing national control of the Egyptian economy.

Harb published two books in response to Qasim Amin's call for the emancipation of Egyptian women: *The Education of Women and the Veil* (Tarbiat al-mara wal higab) was published in 1899, and *The Final Word on Women and the Veil* (Fadl al-khitab fi al-mara wal higab) was published in 1901. In both books he reiterated many of Mustafa Kamel's suspicions, but more forcefully. Harb branded the movement for the emancipation of women as just another plot to weaken the Egyptian nation and to transfer the immorality and decadence prevalent in the West to Egyptian society. He criticized Egyptians who wished to ape the West and claimed that there was a European design to project a negative image of Islam by projecting a negative image of Muslim women. Too many outsiders were trying to meddle in Egyptian affairs, said he, and pointedly mentioned the non-Egyptian origin of Qasim Amin's family.

In the introduction to *The Education of Women and the Veil,* published only a few months after *The Emancipation of Women,* Harb accused Amin of having started an uproar that divided nationalists into two camps. One camp, very small in number, fully endorsed Amin's ideas, but the other camp, which constituted the majority, rejected his ideas. Harb accused Amin of wrongly interpreting the Islamic religion and the intent and content of the Qoran in order to support his feminist cause. The main reason for the strong opposition to Amin's ideas, said Harb, was the deep-rooted feeling among Egyptians that the call for the unveiling of women and the mixing between the sexes was no more than a European fad. A fad, claimed Talaat Harb, that had been instigated by Khedive Ismail, who in his attempts to please the West had been willing to make Egypt part of Europe. Ismail had started the movement for political reasons—namely, to induce the West to help him become independent of the Ottoman Empire. Harb accused Qasim Amin of following the same course and even went so far as to claim that *The Emancipation of Women* did not represent Amin's ideas but was a translation of some articles that had been published previously in English newspapers.

Throughout the remaining parts of *The Education of Women and the Veil,* Harb presented his own views on the nature and roles of women in society, perhaps epitomizing the attitudes and conceptions prevalent at the time. Women, he claimed, quoting the Bible and the Qoran, were inferior to men, physically, intellectually, and morally. If not, why then have women for decades submissively accepted the leadership and supremacy of men?! Women should be educated, he conceded, but if we have to choose between educating men and educating women, then the former should be selected as it is the men who were responsible for the morality of all the members of their households. Women should be educated but only to better perform their natural roles as wives and, more significantly, as mothers. They should be taught first that according to Islam and the Sunna a mother must breastfeed her babies; second, women should be taught morality and the good standards of behavior; and only last should women be taught the rudiments of reading and writing and some general knowledge in math, geography, history, and the other disciplines. On the question of veiling, Talaat Harb was adamant. There was no way that the Qoran or Hadiths could be interpreted to mean that women could go unveiled. The scriptures were clear that women had to be veiled from head to foot and must be kept secluded and protected in their homes from all temptation.

After disclaiming any connection with Amin, *Al-Muayyid* throughout 1899 published a series of articles by Farid Wagdi in response to Qasim

Amin's ideas. *Al-Muayyid* was the mouthpiece of the Constitutional Reform party founded in 1890 by Shaikh Ali Yusif and was the major platform for Muslim conservative Egyptian nationalists. The newspaper was in deadly opposition to innovation or Westernization of any kind. Farid Wagdi, who obviously was conversant with Western thought and knowledgeable about Western society, used all his versatility and knowledge to combat Amin's call for the emancipation of Egyptian women. In Wagdi's first article, titled "A Look at the Emancipation of Women," he draws on history to argue that women are both physically and mentally inferior to men. Have not women since time immemorial been subjugated by men? Have not men been responsible for all great inventions? Women's contributions to humanity, he claimed, have been minor because women's natural roles and inclinations prevent them from devoting time to intellectual matters.

In this and other articles published in *Al-Muayyid,* he goes to great lengths to show that the entrance of women into public life in the West had disastrous effects. In the United States, the number of women who held jobs had increased since 1780, but so, too, had the rate of divorce, so that in that country it was the highest in the world. Sociologists, he said, had studied working women and had concluded that they were no longer women, but a third sex. They were melancholic, lonely, and unhappy beings because to work they had to remain single and had to give up their natural roles as mothers and wives. Women in Europe, he wrote, had acquired many rights, but the police reported that not less than ten thousand women were found each year in the streets drunk and were made to pass the night in police stations. Further, said Wagdi, the West had throughout its history treated women in a barbaric manner. Historical accounts attested to the fact that European women were forbidden to eat, talk, and laugh and were treated like slaves and even less than slaves. Did not one of their prominent thinkers publish a book titled *Do Women Have a Soul?* The movement to emancipate women in the West, claimed Farid Wagdi, was an outcome of the spread of atheism, corruption, and immorality. Are not some women questioning the whole institution of marriage because it deprives them of enjoying sexual pleasures with several men at one time? This movement was the true subjugation of women. The East, according to Wagdi, was more civilized and refined because it respected women's nature and natural inclinations. Was the East to give up its refinement and civilization for the sake of barbaric customs and traditions? Finally, asked Farid Wagdi, how could Egyptians be asked to equate men and women when God did not?!

Qasim Amin's appeal on behalf of the women of Egypt found support from an unexpected quarter during the years 1907–1909 when Malak Hifni Nasif (1886–1918) began to write and speak on behalf of women's rights. As a daughter of Hifni Bey Nasif, a distinguished member of Muhammad Abdu's party (Al-Manar), she was trained according to the more liberal standards held in that circle. After attending various primary schools, she entered the Saniyyah School for female teachers in 1893, graduated at the top of her class, and obtained the government primary certificate in 1900, the first year in which girls sat for that examination. She then continued her studies in the secondary division, receiving a diploma in 1903. Thereafter, she taught in government schools for girls.

There were prominent women in Egyptian public life during her time, among them Aisha al-Taimuriya, a renowned poet. However, such women were of Circassian, Turkish, or Kurdish origin, but Malak was purely Egyptian. Her father started as a modest civil employee, but through diligence and perseverance managed to complete his law studies and embark on a law career. Malak inherited from her father his sense of humor, sarcastic appreciation of life's contradictions, intelligence, humanity, and gentleness. However, she also was known to be very temperamental. She enjoyed elegiacs and read the poetry of al-Mutabani, writing poetry herself and publishing at the age of thirteen. She also had strong nationalist feelings and had she not chosen to be a feminist probably would have distinguished herself as a nationalist heroine (El-Qalamawy 1962). She was obsessed with education, especially the education of women, and went to neighboring homes encouraging families to educate their daughters. She even collected some girls in her home and gave them private tutoring. A philanthropist and benevolent, she tried to help the needy, preferring the company of the poor to that of the well-to-do of her own class.

In February 1907, when she was twenty-one, Abd al-Satar al-Basil Pasha, a prominent member of an influential family of pure Arab stock, asked her hand in marriage. Within less than a month they were married, and she went to live with him on his vast estate in al-Fayyum, on the fringes of the desert. It was from here that she chose her pen name, Bahithat al-Badiya (the Inquiring Desert Woman).

It was really Malak's personal experience with marriage that induced her to take up feminism as her life's cause and to consecrate her life and pen to defending women's rights. Basil turned out to be an incompatible husband who had little respect for the marriage bond. Although he had attested his admiration for her intellect before marriage, she soon found that to him she was no more than "a precious possession to add to his other possessions" and just an annex to his life and home. It also turned out that he already had a wife, whose young daughter he asked Malak to tutor privately. The eleven years she spent with him, her despondency at being a second wife, and the merciless manner in which he imposed his daughter on her ignited in Malak the "sacred fire," as May Ziadah, Malak's close friend and ally, described the pain that induced her to fight for women. She also spoke with and listened to other women in the village of al-Fayyum and in Cairo and became convinced that polygamy was the very worst of all women's ills.

She also began to look at urban life critically and found that ignorance and idleness prevailed among city women and that their relations with their husbands were determined by seclusion, tension, and despotism.

Basil did not seem to object to Malak's work on behalf of women. In her articles and addresses she did not hesitate to deal with many of the problems that Qasim Amin's books had made the subject of heated controversy. Her book *Women's Issues* (al-Nissayat) was first written as a series of articles for *Al-Jarida,* the mouthpiece of the Umma party, and then appeared as a book in 1910. In this book she discussed topics such as "A View of Marriage: Women's Complaints Against It," "Veiling and Unveiling," "Our Schools and Our Women," "Polygamy," "Age at Marriage," "Using Make-Up," "Women's Beauty—Smoking and Drinking," "Women's Beauty—Sports." In the article "Women's Principles," Malak analyzes the faults and weaknesses of women that contribute to unhappiness in the family and failure in marriage; and she does the same for the men under the title "Corresponding Ideas in Men."

It is apparent that Bahithat al-Badiya was influenced greatly by Qasim Amin, yet she declared in one of her poems that she did not belong to his way of thinking. She was more conservative than Amin, repeatedly emphasized her strong allegiance to Islam, and condemned imitation of the West. She called her demands reform rather than emancipation. May Ziadah, the well-known poet and Malak's life-long friend, in a discerning comparison of Malak and Amin, believed Malak to be Amin's daughter in thought and daring and his pupil in advocating reform in women's affairs. Yet, "she walked warily in the midst of the varieties of new thoughts and modern opinions. For every forward step that she took she looked backwards, in order to be assured that she was following the path which connects the past with the future" (quoted in Adams 1933: 237).

Malak, it seems, sought to follow a middle course, preserving as much as possible of current customs. In this and in her public veneration of Islam she may have been an astute politician making a correct assessment of the intellectual atmosphere of the society to which she belonged. As a woman, she was much more vulnerable than Qasim Amin, and she also may have learned a lesson from observing the furor with which Amin had been attacked. She may have been practicing the "art of the possible," which, as we will see later, is a distinguishing characteristic of feminism and feminists in the Arab world.

Malak's conservatism showed itself on the issue of discarding the veil, of which she did not approve. Her disapproval was neither religious nor economic in origin; rather, she objected on social grounds because discarding the veil stood for greater freedom between the sexes, which was not to be desired: "When we study the different classes of society and compare the degree to which the women mingle with the men in each class, we learn for a certainty that the class that mingles most freely is the most corrupt" (Nasif 1910: 9).

Despite her conservatism, Malak was more active than Amin. In 1911, she delivered a famous speech to the Legislative Assembly giving a ten-point program for the improvement of women's position, for which she demanded legislation. Five points concerned education of women: that education should be religiously oriented; that it should be compulsory up to the primary level; that its curricula should include hygiene, childrearing, first aid, and household economics; that a number of women should be trained in the medical and teaching professions to fulfill the educational and physical needs of women; and that all faculties should be opened to women who chose to pursue higher studies. The remaining five points were that girls be trained from childhood in truthfulness, energy in work, patience, and so on; that legal procedures be followed in betrothal, so that no two people could be married without first meeting in the presence of a *mahram* (male relative whom a woman cannot, by Islamic law, marry); that the example of Turkish women in Constantinople be followed in the matters of veiling and seclusion; that indigenous culture be preserved and all imported and alien ideas rejected; and, finally, that men implement all of the above!

These demands were rejected, but Malak continued her agitation on behalf of women. She founded the Union for the Education of Women, which included Egyptian, Arab, and European women among its members. During World War I, she was active in the war efforts and volunteered to sew clothes for the Red Crescent. She also made an effort to contact foreign women who visited Egypt to give them a less skewed image of the lives of Egyptian women. Among the women she contacted was Elizabeth Cooper, author of *The Egyptian Women*.

Malak died, much lamented, on October 17, 1918. A memorial service following her death, at which the minister of education presided, was attended by the leading men of the country, and the list of speakers included not only men of progressive views but also conservative men from the al-Azhar (the teaching mosque and international center of Muslim learning for nine centuries). At the service, words of praise were said of her that had never before been spoken of a women in Egypt.

Another important figure in this first phase of Egyptian feminism was Ahmad Lutfi al-Sayyid. As was to be expected, Qasim Amin found a strong supporter in the founder of the Umma party and editor in chief of its mouthpiece, *Al-Jarida*. Feminism was not al-Sayyid's life cause, but the strong moral and other support he lend Qasim Amin and Malak Hifni Nasif gave them strength and bestowed on their cause some degree of respectability.

Yet with all his progressive reform ideas and independence of thought, Lutfi al-Sayyid retained a moderately conservative attitude when it came to women. His demands for the education of women were not unqualified. He claimed that education for women should not be unlimited—when asked to enumerate the specific fields of study he had in mind, they were home economics, literature, and needlework (Phillip 1978). Malak Hifni Nasif's articles appeared frequently in *Al-Jarida,* yet in his introduction to her *Al-Nissiyat,* al-Sayyid commended her for choosing to follow a moderate course, within the limits of Islam and Sharia.

Another of the prominent supporters of Qasim Amin was Ibrahim Bey al-Hilbawi, doyen of the legal profession, a pupil of al-Afghani, and assistant editor, with Muhammad Abdu, of the *Journal Official.* Al-Hilbawi was a very close friend of Amin, and when the latter, through his books, became known as the champion of women's rights, al-Hilbawi was one of the few who espoused with Amin the "unpopular cause"! After Amin's death, al-Hilbawi continued to fight until he saw a great change in public opinion on the subject.

• THE INTELLECTUAL DEBATE PHASE:
DIMENSIONS AND CONSEQUENCES •

That Qasim Amin chose feminism as the arena to propagate his ideas for social reform in Egypt was no easy matter and required tremendous courage. Even today, male/female relations in Egypt remain a potentially explosive topic. This first stage of Egyptian feminism was probably the most ferocious and conflict-ridden of all the phases. Qasim Amin was up against a "social mythology" that for centuries had divided Egyptian society into a man's world and a woman's world. He was attacking the very fabric of Egyptian society. His arguments touched the very honor, dignity, and moral beliefs of each and every male. Amin's demands were construed as demands for the "underlife" of society to come out of hiding and, to use Elise Boulding's (1975) terminology, claim a share in the "overlife." As members of the "underlife," women were stripped of autonomy, identity, and privacy, and were treated as if they were prisoners, inmates of mental hospitals, or dependent children. Amin was advocating that women were none of these but were first and foremost human beings with equal worth to men. He was advocating that the "underlife" challenge the "overlife" and, to use Evelyne Sullerot's terminology (1968), that the "dedans" (inside) stand up against the "dehors" (outside).

Change is most difficult in the realm of ideas, traditions, customs, and moral beliefs. The adoption of modern technology, an airplane or a plow, is done without much questioning. One acknowledges its existence, learns how to use it, and then uses it. But new ideas, beliefs, and concepts trigger conflict on both the social and personal level. Individuals find their deep-rooted beliefs questioned and put to the test.

The first stage of Egyptian feminism was a conflict about principles, symbols, and issues and as such had none of the requirements that make for ease of resolution. According to game theory, conflicts about material benefits, such as higher wages or the implementation of a project, have calculable costs, are irreversible, and have a non-zero-sum outcome. Conflicts about symbols and issues, such as the status of a group in society or the acquisition of "citizenship status" by a hitherto excluded group, have symbolic and moral values that are not easy to assess. A moral division of labor is not possible, and what one group gains is viewed by the other group as a total loss. The unveiling of Egyptian women implied a questioning of the authority, experience, and ostensibly higher moral level of men. When Amin argued for the emancipation of women as a means for the emancipation of the whole country, to the men it meant a jeopardizing of their status and a challenge to the considerable power they held in the existing social order.

Elizabeth Janeway (1971), in her book *Man's World, Woman's Place,* calls "social mythology" the major determinant of women's status and the major detriment to any change. She defines social myths as "a vast superstructure built on emotion, by desire and fear. . . . Their tenets are declared to be true because members of society feel they ought to be true and they therefore behave in ways that make them true" (p. 10). Social mythology, whose basic tenet is innate sexual separatism, divides human society the world over into a man's world and a woman's world. Social myths are the product of profound emotional drives that are basic to life. Sometimes these drives can act directly and effectively on the world of events. Sometimes they succeed through rationality and logic. But sometimes they substitute action for a will to believe that what is believed exists—or should exist. Examining social mythology is not easy; challenging and changing it are even more so.

The first phase of feminism, because it was part of the move toward Westernization that occurred in cities such as Cairo, was felt strongly among the upper classes, less so among the middle classes, and scarcely at all among the lower, or peasant, classes of late nineteenth century Egypt. One of the earliest outcomes of the British occupation was that it threw into disequilibrium the traditional social balance and disturbed the age-old, well-settled social strata by culturally alienating the native upper class from the rest of the population.

As the centers of foreign cultural influence, social classes were a characteristic of towns and cities, not of villages and nomadic tribes. Before the advent of the British, there was extreme economic inequality between the classes and a big economic gap between the rich and the poor. Yet, economic inequality was a reality that coincided with ideological precepts. According to Islam, the division of worldly goods is willed by God alone. There is even a certain religious virtue in poverty, and the rich are expected to share their worldly wealth with the poor through alms-giving. Despite economic inequality, there was a cultural and moral continuum between the rich and the poor.

When Europeans superimposed themselves as the topmost layer of the upper class, they created a new prestige order and disrupted this cultural and moral continuum (Patai 1955). The native upper classes came to copy and imitate Europeans not only by adopting their technology and gadgets, but also by internalizing their attitudes and morality. The upper class came to regard the lower classes and peasants as primitive and backward, and the gap between upper and lower classes widened, thereby alienating the former and frustrating the latter.

Religiosity had been as much a hallmark of the traditional upper crust as it was of the lower. But among the upper classes those with positive views toward the West adopted a certain lack of concern about their religion. This Westernization indirectly entailed an increasing coolness toward religion as a whole. The most important instrument through which religion exercised its hold on the individual was the traditional patrilineal, patrilocal, patriarchal, extended family. As the individual, especially young male, extricated himself from the hold of religion, he also extricated himself from the hold of his family. He left behind the old, tightly knit family system and was open to ideas of change, such as the emancipation of women and a more egalitarian relationship between husband and wife within a nuclear, rather than an extended, family.

Among the urban lower classes, by contrast, Westernization created greater dissatisfaction. Their consciousness of being disinherited from their ancestral place in society increased their frustration and expressed itself in the eruption of nativistic movements such as the Muslim Brothers and others. Westernization thus paradoxically meant the copying of Western techniques and ways and a decline of religiosity, among the upper classes, but the intensification of traditional hatred of foreigners and religious fanaticism among the lower classes (Patai 1952).

The peasant culture of nineteenth century Egypt was essentially an "illiterate culture," and like other nonliterate cultures, it had a rich storehouse of oral literature—folk stories, popular tales, songs, epics, sayings, and adages—all upholding and feeding the social myths that separated the lives of men from those of women. But more significant than the variants of folk literature were the tenets, teachings, and traditions of Islam, the religion that glued the society together, permeated the totality of life, and held supreme sway over the great majority of the population. This was especially true in the agricultural villages, the unadulterated strongholds of religious traditions (Patai 1952). A deep religiosity was the fundamental motivating force in all aspects and phases of village culture. Religion had its say in practically every act and moment of village life so that a moral code dissociated from religion could not even be conceived. Islam, with the variants of its religious content—elements of pre-Islamic, formal Islamic, and popular *tawaif*—and its interpretations and misinterpretations, left no doubt that women "were inferior beings mentally and spiritually."

The deep religiosity of Egyptian men and women and its strong hold on the majority of the population were the factors that the intelligentsia of the

Egyptian Age of Enlightenment failed to take sufficient note of, and these factors caught most contemporary analysts off their guard when Islam reappeared as a significant force in sociopolitical change in present-day Egypt (Esposito 1980).

One of the factors that prevented the first phase of Egyptian feminism from bringing about any real changes in the position of women was the absence of state support for feminist ideas. The Turkish feminist movement, which bears many similarities with the Egyptian, found a strong supporter in Kamal Ataturk, Turkey's president for more than thirty years. Kamal Ataturk argued strongly for women's equality and full participation in the labor force on the grounds that only thus could Turkey progress. "A country which seeks development and modernization must accept the need for change," he said in a speech in Izmir in 1923. "The weakness of our society lies in our indifference to the status of women" (Ahmed 1984: 114). One of Turkey's major needs, he declared, was "the enlightenment of our women in every field. They shall become educated in science and arts; they shall have the opportunity to attend any school and attain every level of education." Turkey was declared a laic state by 1926, the veil was outlawed, and the Islamic family code abolished and replaced by a civil code modeled on that of Neuchatel, Switzerland. In 1930, women gained the right to vote.

Thus, Turkey was the first Muslim nation to broach feminist issues on a national political level. But although the issue of women and the improvement of their condition was as live among Egyptian intellectuals as it was among their Turkish counterparts, no government, party, or male individual with access to power was to adopt it as a central issue (Ahmed 1984). This was to make a crucial difference to the evolution of the women's movement in Egypt.

Nevertheless, the feminist movement in Egypt ignited feminist debates elsewhere in the Arab world, especially in Iraq and the Levant. Especially during the nineteenth century, when most Arab countries were under the suzerainty of the Ottoman Empire, marriage customs, sex mores, the position of women, and the division of labor, authority, and prestige between the sexes were similar, and in some cases identical from one country to the next. The Iraqi poet Gamil Sadeq el-Zahawi wrote numerous poems in which he reiterated many of Qasim Amin's ideas and demanded the emancipation of Iraqi women and their education. El-Zahawi was forced to leave his job as a consequence, but was later forgiven. In the Levant, strong women's movements were born. Feminists encouraged the "renaissance" of women and gave strong support to women's cultural and philanthropic organizations. Throughout, Qasim Amin was recognized as the leader of these movements, and his ideas were repeated by poets and writers. Finally, Amin's books were translated into foreign languages. In 1912, *The New Woman* was translated into Russian, and in 1928, *The Emancipation of*

Women was translated into German (El-Sakakiny 1965:53).

The first phase of Egyptian feminism came to a halt with the eruption of World War I. With the advent of the war, Egypt was declared a British protectorate. Increased military rule of the country and the events of the war itself temporarily subdued the nationalist and reform voices of the new elites of educated people. During the war discontent accumulated. In the cities inflation hit the lower classes, and in the villages the peasants suffered from such measures as mobilization of draft animals, forced labor, and confiscation of products. The tax burden was increased. The frustration and disaffection of the various classes soon were to explode into the revolution of 1919. But, until then, all intellectual debate of reform, including reform in the position of women, was forgotten. The overriding concern of the whole country was independence from British rule.

CHAPTER THREE

The Nationalist Phase (1919–1924)

Throughout the history of Egypt, chroniclers report that in times of crisis the Egyptian populace invariably resorted to public demonstrations and riots before the authorities to complain of some measure of injustice or to protest against hardship. Historians report that women always formed a part of these demonstrations. Egyptian women of the peasant and lower urban classes had participated in public demonstrations against the injustices of the French expedition and had rioted against the rise in prices and corvée labor during the time of Mohammad Ali. Although women fought for their men's rights, rather than for their own, they nevertheless participated in rioting and demonstrations (Marsot 1978).

The participation of Egyptian women in the 1919 revolution, however, is the event that invariably receives the most prominent coverage by historians. This was the first time in the country's history that *hareem,* upper-class women participated in rioting, when veiled and dressed in black from head to foot, they flooded the streets of Cairo to protest British policy. By 1919, these women could look back on almost twenty years of intense debate on the issue of their emancipation. Now it seemed that this debate was showing its first tangible results. The political roles of these women did not end when riots, demonstrations, and strikes subsided, but continued until 1924.

The historical accounts of the contribution of Egyptian women to wars and revolutions offer portraits of women as martyrs, soldiers, propagandists, and patriots. These portraits rectify the sins of the omission of women in traditional historical accounts and offer images of women as active and heroic, in contrast to their image, implicit in such omissions, as the passive, nonpolitical, timid sex. Yet, going beyond description, the analysis of these historical accounts, of the expectations raised in women by the exigencies of war and revolution, and of the explicit promises made by the leadership who sought women's cooperation has attested repeatedly to the resiliency of traditional roles and structures and the frugality of egalitarian change (Berkin and Lovett 1979). It is in this contradiction between the promise of change during times of crisis and the restoration of tradition after the restoration of normalcy that the participation of Egyptian women in the revolutionary events of 1919 to 1924 is to be located.

In *A Dying Colonialism* (1967), Frantz Fanon predicted that through violence and armed struggle, the condition of women in Algeria, like that of young people, would undergo a revolutionary change. Fanon was referring to the participation of Algerian women in Algeria's struggle against French colonization, a struggle that lasted from 1954 to 1962. The very fact of taking up arms, of participating in violent action, he argued, would lead women to emancipate themselves. Also men, finally convinced of the injustice of women's condition, would support their demands for emancipation in greater and greater numbers. In other words, according to Fanon, armed struggle with no other purpose than national independence by itself should modify mentalities in an irreversible fashion and, in consequence, change the status of women (Mince 1978:159)

Fanon's predictions proved wrong for a number of reasons. First, he did not take into account the motivation and the modalities of women's participation in the Algerian struggle. Throughout the years of the resistance, women indeed played prominent roles. Yet, in the majority of cases, women were utilized, although willingly, as auxiliaries and adjuncts (Mince 1979: 162). Relatively few women entered the battle on their own initiative. Rather, as French repression became more and more severe and as the men had to go underground, they turned over to women tasks they themselves no longer could perform. Especially in the cities, women became active when it became too dangerous for the men to move. This was especially true when the National Liberation Front began to make attempts to bomb French barracks. Protected by the veil and considered by the authorities to be too bound by tradition to participate in such activities, women were able to penetrate into places where it was too dangerous for men to go. Some of these women were arrested, imprisoned, and tortured and were made into "national heroines."

Yet, although the involvement of women was sincere and courageous, their participation occurred mainly on the basis of replacement. It was chiefly in their capacities as wives, sisters, and daughters that they became involved. So, in effect, the participation of women was an emergency measure used to accelerate the process of decolonization.

Second, Fanon ignored the fact that the majority of Algerian militants had no goal other than independence and were extremely vague when it came to envisaging the society they wished to create. In fact, after independence, their adherence to traditions was even more vehement than before colonization. The Algerians wanted to return to the norms, ways of life, and social organization they believed colonization had challenged, if not destroyed. Algerians identified themselves as Arabo-Islamic, and true independence meant the rejection of all moral codes imposed by European society. The idea of the emancipation of women was an alien idea that came with the colonizer (Rowbottam 1974:206–206). True respectability for Algerian women lay in old traditions and customs. After independence, Algerian women were expected to go back to their homes, which they should never have been forced to leave in the first place.

The dichotomy between the egalitarian and rhetorical ideology of revolutions and the reality of women's continued oppression in postrevolutionary societies has been observed by scholars and historians studying other revolutionary movements occurring in different junctures in history and under different social and political circumstances. The French Revolution of 1789, in which women were active participants, gave political emancipation and authority to adult upper-class males. For French women, the institutional changes of the revolutionary decade were more apparent than real. The Napoleonic state that emerged from the French Revolution did not give women political emancipation. Instead, the state reasserted the patriarchal values that had existed in French society for centuries. If anything, French women's public roles were reduced. The Napoleonic Code did not distort the French heritage but provided a more efficient means for controlling women's behavior than preceding regimes had ever accomplished—"old wines were presented in new bottles" (Johnson 1979; Pope 1979).

Similarly, the decisions and attitudes of legislators in the postrevolutionary United States gave little indication that they had internalized the egalitarian ideology of the revolution. Instead, white women found themselves more restricted to the domestic sphere (Salmon 1979). The changes in the lives of women in the USSR, China, and Cuba were not, in these three countries, an immediate consequence of revolutionary movements. In postrevolutionary times, with the structural changes involved in the transition to socialism, transformations in consciousness did not occur automatically or spontaneously. Rather, there was a time lapse between the changes on the structural level and the corresponding changes in superstructure. In all three countries, the gap between ideology and practice, briefly narrowed during the years of turmoil, remained open and grew even wider in the immediate postrevolutionary period (Farnsworth 1979; Maloney 1979; Casal 1979).

Although these five revolutions occurred during a span of two centuries and were rooted in very different social and political circumstances, they had a lot in common. All five fought against one common enemy—despotism; all five had the common goal of reforming their societies along egalitarian, national, and secular lines; and all five were characterized by mass participation in which women played a variety of more or less active roles (Berkin and Lovett 1979:79). Yet, read on another level, these same five revolutions tell a story of disappointed hopes, of betrayed trust, and of oppression—they tell the story of the thwarted hopes of politically sophisticated women denied authority in postrevolutionary societies.

Should one conclude from this that women are manipulated and used by male leaders for as long as women's energies are needed for the success of the revolution and then are cast aside and denied a share of power after the revolution is over? Such a conclusion cannot go unqualified. First, history has pointed repeatedly to the contradictions between ideology and practice. Traditional mentalities are most difficult to modify. Armed struggle can change mentalities only to the extent that it supports a revolutionary ideology that is capable of slicing off from tradition all its social and cultural conservatism and preserving only what can be liberating and adapted to the goals of a new society. The explanation for the exclusion of women from public life and from power in postrevolutionary societies is to be sought in the persistence even in the midst of cataclysmic changes of patriarchal values and of social arrangements unfavorable to women. Male revolutionaries, happy to see women's political activism in times of crisis, are quick to reimpose patriarchal values once the crisis is over. The political activism of women in wars and revolutions is an emergency measure imposed and necessitated by the conditions of revolutionary struggle (Rowbottam 1974:162). Such activism is not intended as nor does it entail a redefinition of women's roles.

Second, women's experiences of revolutionary movements is inherently different from that of men. Women's revolutionary activism arises mostly out of their traditional roles as wives, mothers, and providers of food and services (Berkin and Lovett 1979:82). At first, women feel the pressure of having to perform their traditional functions under conditions of instability and scarcity. Later on, with the scarcity of men, women are called upon to perform the functions that men no longer can perform. Women experience a rapid, dramatic, and stressful expansion of the responsibilities to which they are accustomed and the burden of performing new, ill-defined roles. Yet, even when women become highly politicized, they usually have male sponsors. Women are rarely among the leaders of revolutionary movements, but are often the wives, sisters, mothers, and lovers of male leaders. After the dust settles, women abandon the political sphere altogether or redirect their energies exclusively toward women's issues. However, women's compliance is more complex than a deliberate and callous exercise of power by male leaders over their female allies. Women's self-perception of their roles during revolutionary movements suggests that their participation is directed by their belief that the sought-after revolutionary changes would enable them to function better as wives, mothers, and providers, so that it is possible that women themselves contribute to the preservation of patriarchal values and their rapid postrevolutionary resurgence.

Even then, the participation of women in revolutionary movements widens women's horizons, gives them a taste of freedom, and teaches them techniques of organized struggle. Organized women's movements have been born in the aftermath of nationalist movements. Women's very participation in these movements seems to empower them to henceforth take stands on issues relating to the status of women.

It is within this context that the nationalist activities of Egyptian women in the period from 1919 to 1924 can be explained. This chapter is about Egyptian women as nationalists. This chapter explores the response of Egyptian women to the overriding nationalist needs of the moment; how women took it upon themselves to play a nationalist role; and the nature of this role. Segregation and seclusion had not prevented women from developing a strong sense of belonging to their nation. They expressed this in actions that were contrary to social customs and a "violation" of traditionally respectable behavior. However, acts that were done for the good of the nation were accepted for that reason. Such a motivating force made acts that normally would have been bad or questionable, good and meritorious. A nationalist act was good no matter who the Egyptian was.

The chapter is also about the bitterness of disillusionment that Egyptian women (like women elsewhere) experienced when after 1924 they were excluded from political life. Nonetheless, maybe as a consequence of this disillusionment, women founded and initiated the first organized feminist movement led by women in Egyptian history.

• FACTORS THAT LED TO THE EMERGENCE OF THIS PHASE •

The relationship between this phase of Egyptian feminism and the nationalist movement was by no means a simple or harmonious one. To understand the nature and extent of women's participation one must delve into the conditions that led to the emergence of the nationalist movement itself.

By the end of World War I, Britain had ruled over Egypt for more than a generation. British administration, mainly through the efforts of Lord Cromer, who had remained the consul general from 1882 to 1907, had created an efficient Egyptian administration and initiated a sound fiscal policy for the country. These achievements brought some degree of economic prosperity, and the production of cotton doubled within twenty years. Thus, peasants and landowners felt more secure. By the outbreak of the war in August 1914, the country enjoyed a relatively stable and efficient government, a solvent economy, a greatly increased production of high quality cotton, and some form of a quasi-legislative assembly. British presence, initially explained as a temporary measure, no longer had a convincing raison d'être. Yet, the long-promised independence was not forthcoming; instead, frustration and disillusionment among the intelligentsia were intensified when in 1914, with the outbreak of war, Britain declared Egypt a British protectorate, deposed Khedive Abbas Helmi II, and appointed his uncle Hussayn Kamel as successor. Hussayn Kamel was appointed sultan rather than khedive, thus severing Egypt permanently from the Ottoman Empire.

Increased military rule and the events of the war itself subdued temporarily the nationalist voices of the new elites of educated Egyptians. Yet, if the British for a while believed that this indicated consent to their rule, they soon learned differently (Phillip 1978). The period of 1919 to 1922, when Egypt was accorded a unilateral and, in effect, nominally independent status, was a period of intense political struggle when all forces in the country were consolidated for one purpose: the independence of Egypt from British control.

The leader of the new nationalist movement was Saad Zaghlul, dubbed the "father of Egyptians." As founder of the Wafd party, the best organized mass party in the annals of modern Egyptian history, he dominated the national political scene until his death in 1927. His father was a *umda* (village headman) from Gharbia, and he studied in the village *kuttab* (elementary school). When he joined al-Azhar in 1871, religious reform was in the air. The date, 1871, was important because it was the year Gamal al-Deen al-Afghani came to live in Cairo. Throughout the 1870s, Saad was one of the inner group of al-Afghani's disciples as well as a prominent member of Muhammad Abdu's group of friends.

Saad later studied law, and from the time he was appointed a judge in the Court of Appeals in 1892, he was associated with the ideas of Muhammad Abdu as well as Qasim Amin and Ahmad Lutfi al-Sayyid. Zaghlul's aim, and the aim of his group during that period was to reform in response to the needs of the modern world. He was an effective administrator, but he also aspired to a political career. Appointed minister of education in 1906 and then minister of justice in 1910, in 1913 he resigned his post and stood for elections in the Legislative Assembly (Vatikiotis 1980; Hourani 1960).

In 1896, he had married the daughter of Mostafa Fahmy. Although belonging to the old Turkish aristocracy, Safia Fahmy identified wholly with her husband's role as leader of the Egyptian nation, played a prominent role in Egyptian politics during his life and after his death, and earned the much respected title, "mother of Egyptians."

Poised against notables, aristocrats, and the khedive, Zaghlul's stance led to the establishment of a new national elite able to mobilize popular support in 1919. The war indeed changed the nature of Egyptian nationalism. From a movement of the educated elite it became a movement that at the moment of crisis could command the active or passive support of almost the entire people. The change was due to the new ideas and spirit generated by the war as well as the events of the war itself. The severance of Egypt's ties with the Ottoman Empire and the declaration of Egypt as a British protectorate had intensified nationalist feelings in favor of creating an Egyptian nation with no political ties with any entity greater than Egypt itself.

The followers of Saad Zaghlul were secular liberalists and reformists who subscribed neither to the earlier pan-Islamic sentimentalism of Shaikh Ali Yusif and his collaborators nor to the romanticism of Mustafa Kamel. When Shaikh Ali Yusif and Mustafa Kamel and their followers disappeared from the political scene, they were replaced by prominent writers, journalists, and publicists who expressed views of a definite European secular orientation and who believed in emancipation through secular, liberal reform and through negotiations with the British. The period from 1919 to the end of the 1920s and even 1930s was a period that has been identified as the golden age of liberal thought in Egypt as well as the golden age of Egyptian national identity (Vatikiotis 1980:245–295). Many of the new leaders of the nationalist movement had been educated in Europe, especially in law and the humanities, and subscribed to views ranging from the classical liberalism of the French Enlightenment to British socialism. The kind of ideas expressed in the writings of these leaders questioned traditions more boldly than ever before. Before World War I, Muhammad Abdu and his followers had introduced the idea of change and development, yet in their reformist ideas they considered or sometimes equivocated about the role of Islam and Islamic traditions. The followers of Saad Zaghlul in the 1920s and 1930s boldly emphasized the role of science in the modern world. Influenced by the scientific theories of nineteenth and twentieth century Europe, they did not hesitate to introduce a socioeconomic rather than a religious interpretation of history, culture, and politics. They still defended Islam but were against its verbatim interpretation and against following the letter of the Qoran and Hadiths for every facet of life. Religion was a matter between each person and God, rather than the source for defining the social order or the institutions of community life.

The followers of Saad Zaghlul were not only intellectual secular liberalists and reformers, but also included landowners, financiers, and the incipient industrial and commercial entrepreneurs who represented the nucleus of a nascent native Egyptian national landed and commercial bourgeoisie. The members of this new bourgeoisie had come to realize the relationship between politics and economics, and from 1917, some of them who had been enriched by the war began to invest capital accruing from agriculture in industry and commerce, two domains until then overwhelmingly controlled by foreigners or minorities (mainly Levantines and Jews). For landowners, financiers, and entrepreneurs, legal and social reform without economic strength was useless.

In terms of their social, political, and economic composition, Zaghlul and his followers seemed the group most capable of organizing communal unity in this phase of Egypt's history. Despite their economic rise and advancement in the cities, the members of Zaghlul's group still were identified in origins and social milieu with the group of small propertied farmers in the Egyptian countryside. Thus, the former's chances of organizing countrywide support were better than any other group. As administrators, their knowledge of and influence on the Egyptian civil service, especially the lower echelons, was considerable. As the secular moderate generation of Egyptian national leaders, these men were more readily acceptable to the Coptic minority than any of their predecessors, the extreme nationalist or pan-Islamic groups. Finally, the efforts of Zaghlul's group and its projects for the reform of education attracted aspiring students as well as teachers and intellectuals.

The existence of a colonial situation in any country has direct impact on the rise of political parties, so that the general character and features of political parties in a colonial situation are quite different from those of political parties in politically independent and economically advanced countries. It has been noted that political organizations in countries under colonial rule follow a three-stage development: from pressure or interest groups to nationalist movements and then to political parties (Coleman 1955). Applied to Egypt, the stage of pressure groups belongs to the earlier pre–World War I period. The 1919–1923 period was the stage of the nationalist movement, while the stage of political parties commenced only after 1923 with the introduction of parliamentary life in Egypt (Deeb 1979).

By their very nature, nationalist movements demand changes in the status quo and consequently employ methods of a semirevolutionary nature, such as demonstrations, general strikes, and boycotts, to achieve their aims. Thomas Hodgkins (1961) coined the term *congress* to distinguish between nationalist movements and political parties. While ideologically political parties may express the principles of only their leaders and members, a congress claims to represent the whole nation and to be the embodiment and the expression of the national will. The very term *congress* tends "to imply a nation of universality." Organizationally, a congress usually has a loose structure comprising different organizations with no well-defined relations among them that are conglomerated around a leading or directing committee. The congress tends to have supporters from all sections of the population because the congress attempts to represent the whole nation. In brief, a nationalist movement or congress is characterized by a "universality" in ideology, structure, and social basis.

When the Wafd was formed in November 1918, it was simply a "national" delegation claiming to present Egypt as nation. From then until 1923 the Wafd was a congress type of political organization, a nationalist movement rather than a political party. During these formative years, the Wafd held a "universal" ideology that was intended to encompass the whole of society and therefore all social classes and groups.

In fact, the Wafd party dominated political life in Egypt from 1919 up to the 1952 revolution. As *the* national party, it provided leadership and embraced every social movement in the country. The party's nationalist propaganda was made to appeal to all classes, and it utilized the genuine grievances of some classes to agitate against the British. The Wafd thus formed "organizations" that were attached directly or indirectly to the party's central committee as such or through the secretary general of this central committee. These "organizations" represented three major social groups in society: workers, students, and women.

The Wafd played a dominant role in organizing and unifying unions. The aftermath of World War I witnessed a wave of labor strikes that hit most of the major industries during the years 1919–1921. One of the causes that contributed to this upsurge of unrest and turmoil was the exorbitant rise in the cost of living that immediately followed World War I. Prices rose by leaps and bounds, and the demand for higher wages to match them was a central issue in strikes. Also, as the artificial protection enjoyed during the war ended, the full impact of foreign competition was felt by the local industry. The high profits realized during and immediately after the war were replaced by losses, and employers began to reduce the number of workers they employed. Wafdist leaders played an important role in organizing labor unions, and the Wafd dominated the labor scene throughout most of the interwar period (Deeb 1979b). A labor movement without the Wafd would not have been possible in that era.

It was also the Wafd that converted the student body into a potent political instrument (Abdullah 1985:91–92). Well before the 1919 revolution, the nationalist leader Mustafa Kamel had been the first to encourage students to take an active part in Egyptian politics. Yet, the Wafd organized student activities, and throughout the events of the 1919 uprising, students were active in political agitation and in distributing leaflets and circulars.

In the same way, the nationalism of the Wafd appealed to another suppressed element, the educated women of Egypt. In the heightened enthusiasm of nationalist euphoria, the feminist cause was revived. The Jarida-Umma group had given Amin's feminist ideas strong support, and the Zaghlul-led Wafd, which was initially identified with the Jarida-Umma group, eventually became the only group to espouse feminisim. it was no accident that the heroic days of nationalism also were those when upper-class Muslim women first took part in public life. There were other political parties at the time: the Liberal Constitutional party, the Watani party, and the Socialist party. Yet, the participation of Egyptian women in the anti-British demonstration of 1919 and in political activities up to 1924 was allied closely to the Wafd.

It was through the Wafdist Women's Central Committee that upper-class Egyptian women were given the chance to play political roles. Once the Wafd turned into a political party after the parliamentary elections of 1924, women once again were deprived of playing these roles. Yet, during this phase, feminism became an active organizational concern of women when in 1923, under the leadership of Huda Sharawi (1879–1947), the Egyptian Feminist Union was founded.

· **ANATOMY OF THE PHASE** ·

This section concerns the manner in which some Egyptian women, at the vanguard of whom was Huda Sharawi, were propelled to join the struggle for national liberation. The following pages examine the leadership, social base, organization, and activities of these women. (Unless otherwise indicated, information on the life of Huda Sharawi and the activities of women during this phase is extracted from Badran [1977], Chapters 2 and 3, pp. 47–155.)

Leadership and Social Base

It was in Minya, the ancestral home of her father, Muhammad Sultan, that Huda Sharawi was born. Her father, who came from a family of notables, in time became *shaikh al-balad* (village headman) of his native village, governor of Beni-Suef, president of *Maglis Shura al-Nouwab* (House of Representatives), and a member of *Maglis Shura al-Qawanin* (House of Legislation). At the time of his death in 1884, he owned 4,440 feddans and three mansions. Huda's mother, Iqbal Hanim, was born in the Caucasus. A reticent, stoic woman who exercised great control over her emotions, she suffered a double isolation as a woman and a Circassian. Uprooted from her original culture and leading a secluded and cloistered *hareem* life, she had little opportunity to adapt to Egyptian life.

Huda Sharawi spent her early childhood in the *hareem* of Sultan Pasha and after his death grew up in the care of her mother, Iqbal, and Hassiba, another of her father's widows. In recounting childhood experiences in her memoirs, Huda reveals that she was acutely aware of the fundamentally different treatment she and her brother Omar, three years her senior, received. At an early age, she realized that this was due to their different sex. Although she shared some of the lessons with her brother, her education for the most part was traditional. She was taught Turkish, French, and piano. By the age of nine, she had memorized the Qoran, an unusual accomplishment for a girl.

Despite this, she hardly could read or write Arabic. Her request to be given lessons in Arabic grammar was turned down. It was one thing that she memorize *ayat* (verses) from the Qoran, but quite another that she be able to read and write. The latter was considered inappropriate for a girl because it might give her dangerous knowledge.

Huda, following the ineluctable trajectory of females—a short childhood followed by marriage and immediate adulthood—was betrothed at the age of twelve and married at thirteen. Her husband, Ali Sharawi, the mentor of her family's estates, was in his forties. Huda's betrothal was kept from her. It was only after preparations for her wedding commenced that she was informed of the marriage planned for her. Huda succumbed to the wishes of her elders. Her consent was not free—she simply bowed under pressure.

The early period of her marriage was for her one of fluctuation between joy and anguish. Her husband at times was gentle and understanding, but soon his treatment of her settled into nearly unrelieved tyranny. Also, not too many months after the marriage his former concubine became pregnant, and it was impossible for him to deny the relationship. Huda succeeded in having her way and returned to her family home where she remained separated (but not divorced) from her husband for seven years.

During the separation, she made efforts to enlarge her learning. She resumed piano and drawing lessons but still was not granted permission to learn Arabic grammar. She also tried to expand the borders of her narrowed, prescribed world. She began to meet new people, including a number of European women, but her social circle remained exclusively female. During that time, she met a French woman, Eugenie Le Brun, who was to have a profound impact on Huda's life. Eugenie had married an Egyptian, but decided that "mixed marriages were a big mistake" and separated from her husband. Continuing to live in Cairo, she acted as a guide and mentor to Huda and helped to ease her in the social life of the upper-class female world of the 1890s.

Eugenie began the first women's salon in Cairo. Nazli Fadl already had started her salon, but it was a salon attended principally by men. Eugenie's salon brought together women from inherently different cultures, Arabo-Islamic cultures in which women were segregated and European cultures in which women were integrated to some degree. Egyptian and foreign women began a dialogue on social issues affecting their lives. One such issue was the veil. Among the women who frequented the salon was Aisha al-Taimuriya, the poet and writer. Eugenie encouraged Huda to shed the etiquette and passivity she had learned in the *hareem* and participate actively in the discussions.

However, throughout the separation, Huda remained firmly within the family orbit. Finally, in 1910, when she was twenty-one, she succumbed to pressure and returned to her husband, with whom she remained until his death in 1922. In her memoirs, she maintains a near silence on her relationship with her husband during this period. Instead, she chooses to focus on her role as a mother. She had two children—a daughter, Bothiana, born in 1903, and son Muhammad, born in 1905.

The year 1908 was a significant turning point in Huda's life. In the spring, Qasim Amin and Mustafa Kamel died, and in the autumn Eugenie Le Brun died. There was a period of profound personal grief for Huda and for her brother, who was close to Mustafa Kamel. Huda reveals that a mission to help liberate women from the bondage of the past began to solidify in her and that the memory of Eugenie and the deep admiration she felt for Qasim Amin were a source of inspiration.

Huda's public efforts on behalf of women's liberation began when she organized the first "public" lectures to female audiences, mostly upper-class *hareem* women, on issues of interest to women. It is important to clarify that the word "public," when used in the context of women's activities before 1919, usually means extra-*hareem* but still in a female environment rather than in an integrated public setting. The same year she also participated in the creation of the first philanthropic society run by Egyptian women. The Mabarrat Mohammad Ali al-Kabir came to play an important role in drawing upper-class Egyptian women out of the *hareem* in order to perform social services on behalf of poor women and children. In 1914, Huda initiated still another new project when she helped to found L'Association Intellectuelle des Dames Egyptiennes. This endeavor, like the previous one, was helped along by royal patronage. The opening talk inaugurating the association's program of lectures was entitled, "Quel peut et doit être la rôle de la femme egyptienne dans l'activité sociale et nationale?" (What can and should be the role of Egyptian women in social and national activities?) In that talk Huda said that by engaging in social service projects, women could acquire practical knowledge, their horizons would widen, and their traditionally inward focus would be directed outward as well. Also, such social services would help to bring down prejudice and change the conventional views that women were creatures of pleasure and beings in need of protection.

The beginning of organized, collective activity on the part of women outside the traditional *hareem* setting was extremely significant in itself. In the process of lending assistance to the needy, the sheltered women of the *hareem* indeed proceeded along the course of their own emancipation from lives of idleness and seclusion. Yet, it is difficult to know exactly what impact these activities had upon women. The sense of social consciousness and feminist awareness that might have been produced or sharpened could not be translated immediately into other forms of activity. War soon broke out, which curtailed movements and made new enterprises impossible. The movement toward the liberation of Egyptian women was still to continue for the time being within the traditional social order.

Activities and Organization

Following World War I, Egyptians made moves to gain national independence. On November 13, 1918, Saad Zaghlul, 'Abd al-'Aziz Fahmi, and Ali Sharawi (Huda's husband) met the British high commissioner, Sir Reginald Wingate, to request permission for an Egyptian delegation to go to London in order to present national demands to the British government. However, authorization was not forthcoming, nor did a later appeal to attend the Peace Conference in Paris come to anything. Meanwhile, the three Egyptians began to organize a permanent body, the Wafd, to speak for the nation. After all efforts to present the Egyptian case abroad had been blocked, Saad Zaghlul, the leader of the Wafd, demanded the end of the protectorate and started to voice other nationalist demands as well. When the British authorities were unable to curb the activities of the leaders of the Wafd, whose massive support was continuing to grow, Saad Zaghlul, Ismail Sidqi, and Hamad Basil were arrested on March 8, 1919, and deported to Malta. The following day, demonstrations and strikes of protest, in which Egyptians of all classes took part, broke out in Cairo, Alexandria, and in cities and towns throughout the country. The 1919 revolution had begun.

Egyptian women were quick to respond to events. Huda Sharawi's husband was left at that moment at the helm of the Wafd in Egypt, and she was about to play an active role in political affairs. Assisted by the wives of the exiled leaders and the wives of other politicians, on 16 March, exactly one week after the outbreak of the revolution, she organized the first women's demonstration to protest the arrest of the nationalist leaders.

On that day, upper-class *hareem* women, whose numbers have been estimated at between one hundred fifty and five hundred, poured into the streets of Cairo. Dressed in black, carrying flags bearing the crescent and the Coptic cross, and waving banners with slogans in Arabic and French, the women descended from their *hareem* carriages and started a procession to the legations of the United States, France, and Italy, where the women left written protest. They then proceeded down Qasr-al-Aini Street toward the home of Saad Zaghlul.

As they neared Zaghlul's house, they were circled by British soldiers. The British commandant of the Cairo police appeared on the scene and spoke to the women. Shortly afterward, he departed on the pretext of going to get authorization for their demonstration. The women were kept waiting in the blaze of the Cairo sun for two hours. When he returned without authorization, they had no course but to depart from the scene. Four days later, they organized a second demonstration that met with the same fate.

The women's demonstrations caused the British police to pay serious attention. Considerable precautions were taken by the commandant of police, who had no normal procedures for dealing with women, especially upper-class female demonstrators. Yet, British opposition did not deter Egyptian *hareem* women. As the events of 1919 unfolded, they became increasingly politicized. A nucleus of activists, many of them married to Wafdist leaders, collected around Huda Sharawi. Meeting in *hareems,* mosques, and churches (inviolate places) to exchange information and plan future moves, the women organized demonstrations and sent out written protests. Such acts of agitation continued for the duration of the revolution.

Although the leadership remained among upper-class Egyptian women, women of other classes participated in protests as well. Actresses and members of theatrical companies went out in open carriages shouting patriotic slogans. The famous actress and later founder of one of the most prestigious Egyptian magazines, Rose al-Yusif, recalls the furor of the times, when she and other actresses joined the men in their rounds of Cairo (Al-Yusif 1953). The Saniyya Girls School was for some time the scene of daily agitation on the part of its pupils, much to the alarm of British teachers. Women of the lower classes gathered in the streets alongside men. These women and men furnished martyrs for the nationalist cause.

There also is evidence that the revolution spread to the countryside. In Asyut and Tanta, women engaged in acts of sabotage against the British. Alongside men, women cut off telephone lines, blocked railway passages, and joined in attacks on prisons where detainees were held (Salem 1984).

In the meantime, Huda Sharawi and the activists around her were busy contacting women to convene a mass meeting. On January 12, 1920, they held a nationalist convention attended by some one thousand women in St. Mark's Cathedral. In that meeting the Wafdist Women's Central Committee was formed, with Huda Sharawi as president. The members of the committee were mostly upper-class women, many of whom had taken part in the 1919 demonstrations, and several of them were wives of Wafdist leaders. The formation of this committee, aligned to the still relatively new (at that time, ten months old) Wafdist men's nationalist organization, was an unprecedented move. Never before had Egyptian women organized for political or nationalist purposes.

The creation of the committee was applauded by Wafdist leaders, many of whom had privately urged it upon their wives. According to some sources, the idea originated with Saad Zaghlul because it was opportune for men to draw women into nationalist activities and to use their support and services. For one thing, the Women's Central Committee contributed toward broadening the base of the Wafd's popular support, which was especially important in the early months of its existence. The committee acted as an important communications link in normal and abnormal conditions. Especially when the male Wafdist leaders were removed suddenly from the scene through a widespread wave of arrests and exile, the members of the

Women's Central Committee did all they could to keep information flowing and a stream of protests to the British alive.

The women's committee also afforded women a formal structure within which to conduct their nationalist activities. In 1922, as the British continued to block all roads to independence negotiations and imposed martial law and a protectorate status on Egypt, the committee moved into a period of intense activity. On January 20, committee leaders held a mass meeting in which they agreed upon the chief retaliatory action to be employed against the British: They were to boycott British goods, to withdraw money from British banks, and to have no contact with anyone British—functionaries, doctors, dentists, chemists, and the like. At the same time, they were to support, and encourage others to support, Egyptian industries and banks.

To implement their program, the Wafdist women worked through the newly established women's social services societies. In Cairo, the Society of the New Woman had been established in 1919 and the Society of the Renaissance of the Egyptian Woman and the Society of Mothers of the Future in 1921. Similar societies had been founded in the provinces. Letters preserved from the leaders of these societies indicate that many looked up to Huda Sharawi for guidance and that the links between the provinces and the capital were kept alive, so that in fact the committee's boycott campaign reached a broad section of the population.

Matters suddenly came to an impasse when on February 28, 1922, Britain unilaterally made a move declaring the independence of Egypt. One year later, in March 1923, Zaghlul finally was set free, and on April 19, the Egyptian constitution was promulgated. In the elections held on January 12, 1924, the Wafd gained an overwhelming majority and Saad Zaghlul formed a government.

Article 3 of the new constitution proclaimed: "All Egyptians are equal before the law. They enjoy equal civil and political rights and are equally subject to public duties and responsibilities, without distinction on the basis of race, language or religion" (*Constitution of the Royal Kingdom of Egypt,* Cairo, 1923). Furthermore, articles 74 and 82 granted universal suffrage in electing members of the Senate and the Chamber of Deputies. However, a subsequent electoral law issued on April 30 restricted suffrage to males only. "Half" the Egyptian nation thus was excluded from full participation in the democratic process on the basis of sex alone.

It was a time of considerable disappointment and disillusionment for Wafdist women. Their chagrin was further heightened when on the occasion of the opening of the Egyptian Parliament (with its Wafdist majority), women were not invited and were even refused entry as visitors or observers. With the return of normalcy, women's nationalist contributions no longer were approved or required. Egyptian *hareem* women were expected to disappear once again into their old, quiet, invisible, and dependent lives.

• OUTCOME OF THE PHASE •

The explanation for this turn of events is to be found in the different percep-
tions of national liberation on the part of Egyptian men and women. According to Margot Badran (1977), in the course of nationalist developments, it
became increasingly evident that there was a male and a female liberation
model. Caught up in the overwhelming struggle for national liberation,
Egyptian men welcomed support from all Egyptians, including women. Yet,
male goals were purely political, and their liberation model called for a new,
formal political apparatus for the exclusive use of Egyptians. At the same
time, men anticipated the continuation of inherited social structures and systems with minor concessions here and there to the changing needs of different classes and groups. For women, liberation likewise meant the end of
interference by foreign powers. However, women were equally convinced
that inherited social structures and systems no longer were satisfactory. Oppression was associated both with the power of the foreign occupier and
with the power of men over women. The national liberation model held by
women required a new formal political apparatus as well as a new social
order.

Egyptian women were not the only group disappointed by the succession of the nationalists to power. Saad Zaghlul underwent a deep transformation as the political struggle continued. After he came to power, hours of
reflection came more rarely, and Egyptians and foreigners alike noticed that
he began to speak with another emphasis. He became autocratic, more im-
perious, and even vindictive in his dealings with other leaders. Thus, at an
early stage, the Wafd began to split at the top.

He also did not deal satisfactorily with Egyptian independence. He still
was considered the leader of the nation, but he had come to power only by
compromising his position vis-à-vis the monarch and the British. The stance
of his government in the crisis over the murder of Sir Lee Stack, the sirdar of
the Egyptian Army and the governor general of the Sudan, exposed Zaghlul
as having "sold out to the British." Under the pressure of public opinion, he
resigned on November 23, only ten months after he had formed his government. The following day, a new cabinet was formed, but the Egyptian Parliament was suspended indefinitely.

However, the events of 1919 had had a deep effect upon some Egyptian
women. During the revolution, their consciousness had been intensified
and their awareness of what it meant to be women was sharpened. On the
fourth anniversary of their first demonstration (March 16, 1923), Huda
Sharawi founded the Egyptian Feminist Union. She was elected president.

At first, Huda Sharawi felt that there was no contradiction between her
role as president of the Wafdist Women's Central Committee and her role as
president of the Egyptian Feminist Union. The former was a structure for
nationalist struggle and the latter for feminist and social issues. Yet, follow-

ing the disillusionment resulting from passage of the electoral law, her attitude began to change.

The immediate response of both the Central Committee and the Feminist Union was to picket the opening of Parliament. The two organizations prepared placards in Arabic and French with nationalist, feminist, and social demands. Later, the organizations printed a pamphlet, *Les Revendications des Dames Egyptiennes,* with a list of thirty-two demands and distributed the pamphlet to members of Parliament and to government officials. The demands were a bid for a large-scale overhaul of Egyptian society. They insisted upon an end to subservience to old structures and old authorities, to powerful foreign occupiers in guises new or old, and to the power of the privileged sex.

In the crisis over the murder of Sir Lee Stack, Huda Sharawi, as president of the Women's Central Committee, had published an open letter in *Al-Akhbar* accusing Saad Zaghlul of failing to fulfill his promises and asking him to resign. The publication of this letter led to an irreparable rupture between her and Saad Zaghlul. She thereupon resigned as president of the Wafdist Women's Central Committee and publicly announced the end of all possible further cooperation with Wafd.

> Although the parting of the ways between Huda Sharawi and the Wafd had come over divergence on a specific issue, there was considerable strain under the surface and there were fundamental problems that would have caused the association to have ended eventually. The fact was that from 1923 the Wafdist women had no central, independent or equal role to play in nationalist affairs as far as the men of the Wafd were concerned. The women had been useful in time of crisis and danger when all reinforcements and defensive units were employed. During critical times, and especially in the absence of the male nationalist leaders, the Wafdist women had had an important activist role to play. However, that was not the case in the more normal atmosphere after the return of the male nationalists to the scene. From then on, within the framework of their Women's Committee attached to the men's political party, the women could do little else than act as a strut to that party. It was the function of women to second the policy and actions of the men's party. The promises, implicit and explicit, the Wafd had made to the women in the course of their nationalist struggle to draw them into the life of the nation once independence was achieved, were conveniently forgotten by the men (Badran 1977:153).

The women did not forget these promises. In fact, the women felt that their participation in the national movement had given them certain claims on the nation, and they intended to see these claims realized. Women concluded, however, that men were not going to bring women into the full life of the nation. They had to assume that task themselves. From the end of 1924 onward, Huda Sharawi turned her full attention to the Egyptian Feminist Union.

CHAPTER FOUR

The Social Activism Phase
(1924–1950s)

Social movements consist of activities directed toward establishing a new order of life. As such, social movements are made up of attempts to change certain existing values and beliefs. Yet, social movements can be either general or specific. A *general* movement aims at an overhaul of society, changing values and creating new ones, but its goals are diffuse and its organization loose. A *specific* movement also attempts to change values, but, by contrast, its goals are more specifically defined, and it contains a "we consciousness" resulting from people identifying themselves with these specific goals and mobilizing to reach them (Snyder 1979).

Although it is difficult to pinpoint when a social movement ceases to be general and begins to be specific or vice versa, the women's movement in the United States in the 1840s is an example of a general movement transforming into a specific one. In the 1700s and 1800s, the women's movement was a general movement that aligned itself with other movements (certain religious movements and the abolitionist movement, for example) taking place at the time. As participants in these movements, U.S. women believed that fighting for the rights of others would help women obtain their own rights. They soon discovered, however, that this was not the case. It was a bitter blow for U.S. women to be told by legislators after the Civil War that their attempts as women to be included in the Fourteenth and Fifteenth Amendments, which extended constitutional rights to blacks but not to black women, were blocking the passage of the amendments. This caused U.S. women to concentrate on their own condition. They held meetings and conventions at which they discussed their suffrage rights and the paths to follow to gain these rights. A small but elaborate social network emerged that engaged in a considerable amount of mobilizing activity, and women's organizations, with different activities but all sharing the goal of obtaining the vote for women, were formed. This brought into full force the specific phase of the U.S. women's movement (Flexner 1970).

This specific period of the women's movement continued until the 1920s when the Nineteenth Amendment gave U.S. women the right to vote. After the passage of this amendment, the women's movement returned to the diffuseness of a general movement, with a marked decrease in mobilization efforts as women's organizations lost membership or ceased to exist (Snyder 1979).

The Egyptian feminist movement in its social activism phase is another example of a specific movement that emerged from a general, more diffuse one. Egyptian women, who had during the nationalist struggle aligned themselves with men as a mere annex to their organization and identifying totally with their goals, after the subsiding of nationalist fervor turned all their efforts to struggling for their own cause. During this period, the Egyptian feminist movement finally crystallized into a movement with a more defined set of goals and a "we consciousness" emanating from various mobilization organizations. An anatomy of this phase of Egyptian feminism is in order.

At the outset, it is important to point out that during this phase of Egyptian feminism, which covers the period from 1924 to 1952, three types of feminists emerged: the "agitators," the "social reformers," and the "pioneers." The agitators were women who engaged in activities and were members of organizations whose immediate aim was to agitate for the rights of women. Huda Sharawi, working through the Egyptian Feminist Union, is representative of this type of feminist. The social reformers were women who through philanthropic women's organizations engaged in social welfare activities. These were women who set an example of what women could do in responding to the social welfare needs of society. The pioneers were women who did not belong either to feminist organizations or to philanthropic societies, but by their individual attempts to penetrate into the public domain paved the way for other Egyptian women to do the same.

• THE AGITATORS •

Huda Sharawi and other women began to call themselves feminists after 1923 and after the founding of the Egyptian Feminist Union. The union was founded in order to form a delegation to represent Egyptian women at the Ninth Congress of the International Women's Suffrage Alliance in Rome in May 1923. The initial contact between Egyptian women and the alliance had been made in 1911, when the president of the alliance, Carrie Chapman Catt, on tour of Eastern countries to investigate the conditions of women, visited Egypt and met with Huda Sharawi, Malak Hifni Nasif, and others (Badran 1977:157–163).

The first years after its founding, the membership of the EFU greatly increased so that by 1929 it claimed two hundred and fifty members. The women who joined were, like Huda Sharawi, predominantly from the upper class, and the character of the EFU was clearly marked by that fact. Coming from large landowning families, these women were of immense wealth and leisure with a Western-type education obtained in the *hareem* or in private foreign schools. In language and manner, these women were French-styled, and the female social world within which they moved included Westerners. The founding members included Christians, but Muslims were in the majority (Badran 1977:157–163).

That the beginnings of a feminist consciousness should come among this class of Egyptian women, traditionally the most secluded and segregated in the whole of Egyptian society, may seem ironic and contradictory at first glance. However, considering the social stratification existing at the time, a serious and sustained movement with any real possibilities of success had to "come from the top." As mentioned earlier, a certain amount of education and exposure to alternatives through contact with other cultures was needed for these women to begin questioning their traditional roles, positions, and lifestyles. These opportunities existed only for the women of the upper classes. Both their wealth, which made travel abroad possible, and their Western-type education induced them to question the existing social order (Phillip 1978). Further, as socially esteemed members of old upper-class families, these women had a better chance of initiating new practices, ideas, and values and a better chance of making such changes respectable and in principle acceptable for all women. In addition, the private wealth of these women gave their movement a certain financial base that eliminated the necessity of compromise in order to stay alive. Finally, still another way in which upper-class origin was important was the access to information, power, and contacts that these women had through their husbands, fathers, sons, and brothers.

The women of the EFU became feminists when they developed a consciousness that as women they were an entity apart, sharing common problems and hence common goals. These goals were to overcome women's "disadvantaged status" by achieving equality with men in both the private and public domains. But like Qasim Amin, these women believed that the achievement of their goals would benefit the whole of society. As functional parts in a society in need of reform, EFU feminists legitimized their demands by the needs of society, not by their own needs as individuals (Phillip 1978).

The type of feminism espoused by the members of the EFU feminists is evident in the goals of the union, as detailed in *Les Revendications des Dames Egyptiennes*. The thirty-two demands included in this pamphlet were divided into feminist demands, social demands, and political demands. The feminist demands called for the education of women, a change of the Personal Status Law, and suffrage. The social demands included improved education, health, and moral standards, upgraded agriculture, and expanded industry. As for the political demands, they were the unconditional independence of Egypt. Couched in these terms, the EFU demands implied that despite women's disillusionment with male national leaders, they still believed that their own independence and emancipation were linked closely to the independence and emancipation of the country to which they belonged.

The EFU's stance on the position of Egyptian women was made public through Huda Sharawi's many addresses and speeches. In Rome, at the Ninth Congress of the International Women's Suffrage Alliance, she elaborated two themes: first, that the position of women in Pharaonic times, when Egypt was at the height of its glory, was equal to that of men and that it was only when the country fell under foreign domination that Egyptian women lost these rights; second, that Islam, too, had granted women equal rights with men, but with the passing of time and through the misinterpretation of the Qoran, women had been usurped of their lawful, equal status with men.

Not all Egyptian women had lost, however, only the few thousand women living in the chief towns of Egypt. Again like Qasim Amin, Huda Sharawi glorified the life of Egyptian peasant women when she said:

> Let us note here that the Egyptian peasant woman still enjoys all her social rights: she goes out with her face uncovered, participates with her husband's purchases and sales, and has a clear idea of agricultural affairs. Man often resorts to her advice, so convinced is he that she is possessed of more wisdom than himself (quoted in Badran 1977:164).

It was the duty of the Egyptian Feminist Union to retrieve the lost rights of urban upper-class Egyptian women. These rights included educational opportunities, changes in personal status laws, and suffrage.

During the 1920s and 1930s, members of the EFU were active in seeking to increase education for women and in urging the government, with some success, to provide free public education for girls. In part, EFU efforts secured women's entry into universities (Ahmed 1984). During the same period, the EFU campaigned for legal reform of family law. The campaign consumed much of the union's energy but without any significant success. EFU demands included the restriction of marriage age, polygamy, and divorce, the abolition of *biat-al-ta'a* (house of obedience), and the reform of custody and inheritance laws. In seeking the legal reform of Sharia laws, members of the EFU made it explicit that they, although feminists, were Muslim feminists. They were fighting traditions and male interpretation of Islam, not Islam, and were against the path that Turkey had followed in secularizing family law.

The concentration of the energies of the EFU members on legal reform proved disappointing, and during the entire duration of their movement under the leadership of Huda Sharawi, there was only one major revision of the Personal Status Law, which occurred in 1929 (Badran 1977). The minimum age for marriage had been raised to sixteen in 1923, and the 1929 revisions only extended the period of the mother's custody over her children and made certain clarifications regarding women's right to demand annulment of marriage. Compared to the EFU demands, these revisions were minimal.

As to suffrage rights, the women of the EFU had made their first public stand on the issue when the new Egyptian Parliament had opened in 1924. After the split between Huda Sharawi and Wafdist leader Saad Zaghlul, disaffection and disillusionment had spread among the ranks of the women in the EFU. Their argument for political rights for women was that suffrage had been granted by the electoral law on the basis of age and sex, with no property or literacy qualifications required of voters. These women protested that ignorant and illiterate men had been granted the right to vote, while educated women were denied this right. These agitators furthermore pointed out the inconsistency between the access to full civil rights accorded them by Islam and their total exclusion from political rights and protested that this was a violation of logic and justice. Moreover, they stressed that women had all the duties and obligations of Egyptian citizens; for example, women paid taxes and were liable before the law and consequently should enjoy all their civil rights. Egypt belonged to all Egyptians and not only to male Egyptians, and suffrage rights should be universal, without distinction of sex.

After the break with the Wafd party, the members of the EFU for some time maintained close relations with the Liberal Constitutional party, whose leaders seemed sympathetic to many of EFU's demands. However, members of the EFU got caught up in the struggle for legal reform and further gains in women's education. Accordingly, in 1926, they announced that for the time being their active quest for female suffrage would be postponed.

The feminism of members of the EFU as articulated in their goals and exemplified by their activities accepted many of the precepts forwarded by Qasim Amin. EFU members accepted his axiom that the Egyptian nation was backward because its women were backward, and accordingly, if the nation were to advance, its women also must advance. However, the membership also followed the path of many of the nineteenth century religious reformers, such as Muhammad Abdu and Rifai el-Tahtawi. EFU members authenticated their feminist objectives on the grounds that they were reclaiming their usurped Islamic rights or that, at the very least, Islam did not disapprove of their objectives. They were adamant in stressing their adherence to Islam and made efforts to be seen as absolutely and irreproachably "correct" in their position with respect to their religion. They projected the image of learned Muslim women revered in their piety and uprightness and set themselves up as models for the new "Muslim" woman. No doubt, this "conservatism," even decorousness, was essential for at least some of their demands being granted. Their stance may have been a matter of political expediency and a demonstration of their astuteness in practicing "the art of the possible" (Ahmed 1984; Woodsmall 1956).

Although the EFU in its lifetime did not accomplish most of its goals, its members contributed to the "liberation" of Egyptian women on a number of levels, mostly by precedent-breaking acts (Badran 1977). Early in the movement, in 1923, Huda Sharawi, upon returning from the Ninth Meeting of the International Women's Suffrage Alliance in Rome, had publicly removed her veil, thus setting an example for other upper-class women to follow suit. Although the percentage of women who were veiled was really minimal, the idea of the veil much more than its material presence was significant. The veil was a symbol of women's seclusion and relegation to a private world and a symbol of their passivity and even invisibility in the public domain. The presence of the veil, especially among the elite, to whose status and mores others aspired, meant nationally that the society was surely riven in two and that women in practice and on the ideal level were nonparticipant, passive, and invisible (Ahmed 1984). As Huda Sharawi herself comments: "La voile, pourtant si leger, etait la plus grand obstacle a la participation de la femme dans la vie active" (The veil, even though so light, is the most serious obstacle in the face of the participation of women in public life) (quoted in Badran 1977:167).

The EFU also was active in a larger-than-Egyptian context. In the 1920s, when the EFU aligned itself with the International Women's Suffrage Alliance, the spirit of international feminism was high. Feminists thought in terms of the universal woman and the universality of feminism. Women, as women, no matter what society or culture they came from, had essentially similar problems and, therefore, similar goals. Newly proclaimed feminists, like the members of the EFU, could learn organizational methods and tactics from women with long histories of feminist activism behind them. The international links of the EFU were clearly reflected in the pages of its mouthpiece, *L'Egyptienne,* started in 1925 (Badran 1977). Its content emphasized the universality of women's problems and told upper-class Egyptian women and European women that they were the same or could be.

However, by the 1930s the members of the EFU came to view the alliance as a Western movement. This shift in perspective came about as a result of the attitude of the alliance to the Palestinian question. The nationalist movement in Palestine provoked a profound change in the Egyptian feminist movement and caused the members of the EFU to redefine their frame of reference. Their nationalism came to be articulated in Arab rather than Egyptian terms, and their feminism then was cast in an Arab rather than a Western context. It became increasingly clear to feminist leaders that to accomplish their goals, it was necessary for them to address themselves to both their Egyptian as well as Arab hinterland. In 1937, *Al-Misriyya,* a bi-monthly Arabic magazine, replaced *L'Egyptienne* as the mouthpiece of the EFU. The new magazine reflected the shift in the feminist movement, emphasizing in its content what was specifically Egyptian, Arab, or Muslim. The magazine's aim was to help Egyptian women develop within their own religious and cultural framework and the masthead stated, "Take half your religion from Aisha" (Aisha was one of Prophet Muhammad's wives, who after his death rose to such a position of respect and esteem that she came to be considered a highly reliable source in the interpretation of the Qoran and the Hadiths).

By the end of the 1930s, the Arab link was fast becoming the most important external link for the EFU. It still retained its membership with the alliance, but its links with Arab women and its desire to develop an Arab feminism became paramount. Finally, in 1945, encouraged by Egyptian men for their own political aims, the members of the EFU played a leading role in founding the All Arab Feminist Union.

The EFU also promoted the birth of a new activist organization, the Bint al-Nil (Daughter of the Nile) organization, founded by Doria Shafiq in 1949. Doria Shafiq, a protégée of Sharawi, set up an action program for her organization that included dramatic measures such as a march on Parliament in April 1952 and a hunger strike of leaders in 1954 demanding that women be included in framing the constitution. The 1952 demonstration provoked al-Azhar to respond by issuing a declaration prepared by a committee of shaikhs stating that women were unfit for the vote on the grounds that they "are swayed by emotion and are of unstable judgement. Whereas men are impartial and balanced, women stray from the path of wisdom even when they have the advantages of good education." However, the Bint al-Nil organization continued its agitation for women's suffrage through publicity and propaganda in the press and radio and through the articles of its mouthpiece, *Bint al-Nil.* It is likely that the organization's activities were directly responsible for Egyptian women's final acquisition of suffrage rights in 1956 (Woodsmall 1956).

For the duration of the social activism phase led by Huda Sharawi and the EFU, there was no notable, articulate opposition to EFU activities as such. The real opposition was the huge, oppressive deadweight of centuries of accumulated custom and attitudes. Those who opposed the Egyptian feminist movement in the social activism phase had so much on their side that in a sense there was no need to articulate an antifeminist case. This phase did not attract the kind of opposition and disapproval that had greeted the books of Qasim Amin, so that there was an absence of "proper" enemies. Also, side by side with the feminist agitators, there were the "social reformers" who in many ways were part of the establishment and who managed to bestow an aura of respectability and acceptability on Egyptian feminism and feminists during this phase.

• THE SOCIAL REFORMERS •

During the social activism phase of Egyptian feminism, a less glorified but maybe more concrete contribution to Egyptian feminism was made by the social reformers. These women also came into public life because of the 1919 revolution, but once the revolution was over, they channeled their talents into setting up philanthropic organizations. The organizations they initiated cover the large majority of social services in Egypt today.

There was a revolutionary social concept in the involvement of upper-class *hareem* women in philanthropic organizations. Although past philanthropic organizations had been financed by *hareem* women, they had never before been actively involved in their activities. By literally rolling up their sleeves and actively taking a hand in the projects of these organizations, these women introduced a number of salient innovations into the practice of assisting the poor and the needy. The dispensing locus was shifted from private houses or from facilities run as *waqf*s (endowments) to the premises of the philanthropic society. These were usually located in the midst of poor city quarters, so that the members of philanthropic societies were brought into contact with the people they helped in a new way. Where in the past it was the norm for the poor to go to the rich, with the new arrangement the rich went to the poor and came to see the social context of their problems (Badran 1977). The philanthropic society was also a collective effort. Its members could be Muslim, Christian, and Jewish. Because their opponents were not the establishment but ignorance, disease, poverty, and apathy (much tougher opponents than any establishment could muster), these women all joined forces to lick the enemy. Charity thus was removed from a specifically religious context and became a civic obligation and, in a larger sense, a national duty (Marsot 1978).

The activism and achievement of the social reformers thus rank with those of the agitators, because these activities were directed toward benefiting the whole of society. Marsot (1978) dubs them the "revolutionary gentlewomen." There was something fine and inspiring about a group of women, such as the members of the EFU, fighting the political establishment—in effect their own husbands and relatives—to gain recognition of their political rights, their rights to equal education and to equal status before the law. Their agitation was the lifeblood of the feminist movement. By contrast, the social activists were not agitators or overt exponents of feminism. They did not antagonize or fight the establishment, but on the contrary were encouraged by it. But by endowing charitable institutions and by helping the less fortunate, the social reformers created monuments to women's constructive and creative power. Through the reform organizations, the social reformers became unpaid public servants, proving by example the equality of the sexes (Marsot 1978).

Following the 1919 revolution, the number of philanthropic organizations run by women greatly increased, but perhaps the most well known of them was the Mabarrat Mohammad Ali al-Kabir. The founder of this organization was Hidaya Afifi (1898–1969), daughter of Ahmad Pasha Afifi, the palace magistrate. Hidaya was educated in the French convent of Notre Dame de la Mère de Dieu, withdrew at puberty, and a few years later married Bahieddine Barakat, a professor at the faculty of law and the son of a Cairo University leading Wafdist, Fathallah Pasha Barakat. Through her family connections and her marriage, Hidaya was from the outset in the center of political activity. As a member of the Wafdist Women's Central Committee, she actively participated in the 1919 uprisings and boycott campaigns.

Gifted with indefatigable energy, a clever and quick mind, and the power to manipulate people, Hidaya developed links with the palace ladies through her father's functions in the palace. Two princesses had organized a philanthropic group that in 1908 set up a small clinic in the Abdin quarter. Unfortunately, these women only met once a month and were not very effective. When Hidaya joined the organization later on, she convinced a large number of her equally activist friends to join it. The Mabarrat Mohammad Ali thus came into existence and grew into the largest and most active women's organization in the country. The small clinic in Abdin blossomed into a full-fledged hospital and out-patient clinic, and a network of similar installations was created. Hidaya, who was treasurer of the association, ran the Mabarrat with the help of the women who were on the central committee. A wealthy and generous princess was chosen as a figurehead president, a title that later went to King Faruk's sister, Princess Fawzia.

The same group of women then set up a second organization to deal with a different set of problems. The Société de la Femme Nouvelle was created in 1919. Where the Mabarrat was to deal mainly with clinics, dispensaries, hospitals, and problems of health, the Femme Nouvelle was to concentrate on aspects of social welfare, like setting up schools where girls were taught a trade, child care centers, orphanages, and so forth.

Both these organizations were financed by donations from the members and their friends, by sweepstakes, bazaars, and dances. The members of the organization were the women of the elite upper classes, both urban and rural, from aristocratic and large landowning families; the women came from all religious denominations and political persuasions. Whether their men were in power or in the opposition, the women cooperated and succeeded in always finding a member who was connected to the government of the day and who would help cut the red tape or obtain government sanction for some project. "Perhaps," writes Marsot, "that is one reason these women were more successful in their projects than their husbands were in running the country." When the women had a project planned, they would talk large landowners into donating a plot of land on which the women wished to build a clinic or dispensary. Next they would seek the *umda* and impress upon him the importance of the project to the village and to himself. The villagers sometimes cooperated in building the dispensaries, so that these ventures became community projects. In some cases, neighboring villages sent delegations requesting that they, too, be assisted in building their own "clinics" or dispensaries.

Disease and hygiene were, and still are, a major problem in Egypt, which was why the Mabarrat expended its energies in that direction. By 1961, the Mabarrat had created twelve hospitals that had treated 13 million patients and were frequently the only medical installations in some territories.

The government, which was impeded by limited budgets and unmotivated personnel, was delighted with the creation of these much-needed projects. Since that time, there has been a steady growth in women's organized efforts to meet the social needs of Egypt. Women's activities have covered a wide range of social services including charity and relief, health and child care, education, economic development, youth service, and village welfare. The expansion of women's organizations was particularly marked after the 1940s when their outstanding services during the war to the thousands from bombed areas and in the national disaster of three epidemics in 1942 and 1947 brought women the recognition of Parliament and the nation. This had a great effect and was a turning point in the progress of women's organizations. The postwar period accelerated their development because of the increased need and opportunities for service. By the early 1950s, there were 156 women's organizations in Egypt (Woodsmall 1956:36). All their projects were supported enthusiastically by the government. Sometimes they were even jointly planned and financed.

The social reformers, like the agitators, were mostly upper-class *hareem* women. Perhaps the social reformers were sublimating their energies into constructive work when they were unable to join in other public activities; perhaps they had more of a social conscience than men and felt that it was not enough to give money; perhaps, like Hidaya, these women were born organizers. Yet, their activities, like those of the agitators, changed the lives of Egyptian women. Husbands and fathers who would have objected violently had their wives and daughters taken paid positions as hospital administrators were shamed into acquiescence by the very fact that the positions were unpaid and for a benevolent cause to which the men had been forced to subscribe funds. Mothers who would have been horrified had their daughters suggested that they train as nurses, accepted the fait accompli of their daughters' nursing the poor as an act of philanthropy, as a religious duty, and as a national duty. Activist women belonged to the elite, for it was their class of women who needed emancipation the most. When these women took up public functions, they made social work respectable. By extension and in time, all work, paid or unpaid, became respectable.

• THE PIONEERS •

The third type of feminists that emerged in this phase of Egyptian feminism were the pioneers. These were women who belonged neither to the agitators nor to the social activists. This third group included women who struggled as individuals to change the course of their lives, thus paving the way for other Egyptian women to do likewise. An example of the "pioneers" is Sohair al-Qalamawy.

Sohair al-Qalamawy was born on July 20, 1911, in one of the fashionable residential areas of Cairo in the district of al-'Abbasiyya. Her father was a surgeon and was therefore, as he put it himself, a member of the upper classes by virtue of education not wealth. A first generation Cairene (his parents were ordinary village people), he underwent great hardship to complete his medical studies at Al-Qasr al-'Ayni Hospital. Sohair remembers him as a "loving, tolerant and kind man" of whom she was very fond. When she was young, she often helped him in his clinic and dreamed of becoming a surgeon.

Her mother was of Turkish descent, a cultured woman by the standards of the time, as she had studied French and Italian in foreign missionary schools. Sohair recalls that her mother had a very strong personality and that her father gave in to her in all spheres, except his work. "My mother often beat us, which we naturally didn't like very much. When I married and had children of my own I developed another attitude toward my children—they were the masters of the house . . . until they too eventually married and established their own families" (personal interview with Dr. Qalamawy, January 1980).

Yet, Sohair al-Qalamawy dedicated her first book, *Tales of My Grandmother,* published in 1935, to her mother with the following words: "To the person who made someone out of me: to my mother."

At the age of four, Sohair went to the American Girls College, one of the few girls schools in the country at that time. Her early contact with Western culture did not alienate her from her own. *Tales of My Grandmother,* which describes lifestyles in the latter part of the nineteenth century in Egypt, shows her strong nationalistic feelings. She describes the Egyptian army as a "tied-down helpless lion in a cage; it cannot even roar" and deplores Britain's strategy in running the educational system in Egypt. "Britain has moulded the educational system in Egypt to produce people of the caliber it needs, i.e., people who do not care about Egypt, alienated people" (Al-Qalamawy 1935:32).

From the same book (Al-Qalamawy 1935), it is obvious that Sohair was taking her education much more seriously than was common at the time. She was chided by her grandmother for reading too much.

Listen to me, my child, and take my advice. Leave these books and you will see the improvement in your health. This habit of reading is an ailment which women of my generation did not suffer from. Bless our good old times! I never allowed my daughters enough time a day to read. Free time only brings devious ideas and thoughts in the minds of girls. Reading to me is like doing nothing. I never let my daughters read a book that their father or elder brothers had not read before them. What a difference between your generation and ours. All these public libraries open to you where you can read anything that pleases you. You already know more than I ever knew or would even like to know (p. 62).

Upon completing secondary school, Sohair wanted to realize her dream and become a medical doctor like her father but could not. The founding of the Egyptian University in 1908 had been made possible partly through considerable material backing from Princess Fatma, a daughter of the late Khedive Ismail. When it first opened, a small number of girls, mostly foreign residents in Cairo, attended classes, and separate facilities were made available for them. In 1925, the university was reorganized and upgraded, from which time it was known officially as Fuad I University. The new charter proclaimed that the university was open to all Egyptians, but many members of the faculty and public opinion in general strongly opposed the entry of women. Fortunately, there was support for women at the top. Ahmad Lutfi al-Sayyid was rector of the university. He favored the admission of women students and embarked upon a practical course of action that was backed by some of his colleagues, including Taha Hussain, who taught Arabic literature and later became the dean of the faculty of arts. Ahmad Lutfi al-Sayyid simply went ahead and allowed a few qualified women to begin their studies. In 1929, the first five Egyptian women students were admitted; Sohair al-Qalamawy was one of them.

Sohair recalls the story of her admission into the faculty of arts rather than the faculty of medicine as she desired. The dean of the faculty of medicine had refused to admit her, although her academic record was exceptionally good—there were to be no female students in his faculty. Furthermore, her parents would not allow her to travel to Europe unescorted. Meanwhile, a friend of the family introduced her to Taha Hussain, who at the time was dean of the faculty of arts. In the conversation that ensued, Hussain told her, "Why do you want to study medicine? The Department of Arabic will teach you anatomy—haven't you heard of Jarir and al-Faraydaq? You will find all the parts of the body there." He then added, "You have a choice between [studying Arabic literature] or staying at home." She chose the first alternative.

Sohair al-Qalamawy is remembered and often cited as one of the first women to enter and graduate from Cairo University. Her graduation, with her other four colleagues in 1933, is considered a landmark in the development of the Egyptian feminist movement in Egypt.

After graduation, she had other problems to face. Her father, who had always backed her in her attempts to realize her ambitions, had passed away. She wanted to work, but as she was twenty-one, according to tradition already an advanced age for an unmarried girl, her mother wanted her to marry. Also, economically they were well-off, and her mother objected staunchily to her working. Women of her class already had come out of the household into public social service. However, volunteer work in philanthropic organizations had an entirely different meaning compared to salaried employment. Women of the lower classes worked in small factories or in other forms of manual work. But lower-class women worked because of dire need, and their paid labor was looked down upon by Egyptian society. For women of aristocratic or even middle-class families, any paid work was degrading.

Sohair managed to have her way, arguing that she "worked not to make money, but because she wanted to work." From 1933 to 1937, she was a freelance journalist and wrote for magazines such as *Al-Rissala* and *Apollo*. She also worked in radio and was the first female voice to speak through this medium. Taha Hussain, who had been forced to leave Cairo University because of his political views, was working for *Al-Wadi* and *Kawakeb al-Sharq* and helped her to publish in these two newspapers. In 1937, she was offered a four-year scholarship to study in France. In 1941, she completed her dissertation on *One Thousand and One Nights* and returned to Egypt. Her dissertation was published in 1943 and won her a first prize from *Al-Majma al-Lughawi,* "The Institute of Immortals" that comprised master scholars in Arabic. In 1942, she took up a teaching post at the Department of Arabic at Cairo University. Many students attended her classes; some came out of genuine interest and others to observe the new phenomenon of a woman teaching male students. The latter sometimes tried to make her job difficult, causing as much commotion and disturbance in class as possible. She says of this experience: "Those first years were very trying. I remember well that the tension made the tears come to my eyes daily as I crossed the Cairo University bridge on my way home" (personal interview with Dr. Qalamawy, January 1980).

Through perseverance and the mastery of "her trade," Sohair al-Qalamawy eventually became a full professor in the Department of Arabic Literature and came to occupy the same position as head of this department as had her early protagonist, Taha Hussain. She also was the first woman to receive the state's prize in literature and the arts in 1977. From 1967 to 1971, she was the chairperson of the General Organization for Publishing and Editing. Upon retiring from that post, she ran for and was elected a member of Parliament.

As a literary figure she is prominent in the literary world as the author (and translator) of a long list of books, numerous articles, and short stories. Today she is a member of the High Council of Arts, Literature, and Humanities, vice-president of the Egyptian Society of Writers, and a member of the Board for Arab Writers Union and the Afro-Asian Writers Union. Married to Yehya al-Khashab, a renowned scholar of Iranian civilization and literature, she has two sons, the elder an engineer and the younger a physician.

This brief sketch of the life history of Sohair al-Qalamawy shows the difficulties and agonies that the first "professional" woman faced in Egyptian society. Not all women who occupy leading public offices are feminists. Nevertheless, as a result of the problems they meet or the obstacles they overcome, such women either become feminists or are thought to be so. Sohair al-Qalamawy was a product of both. She became a symbol of feminism through her own inherent talents and her pioneering lifestyle. She also became secretary-general of the All Arab Women's Federation in 1966. Today she is considered one of the leading feminists in Egypt. According to *Al-Hilal* (April 1978), she is cited as one of four women who contributed to the feminist movement. Huda Sharawi, president of the EFU, Safia Zaghlul, wife of the Wafdist leader, and Amina al-Said, editor in chief of one of the leading women's magazines and one of the first women to graduate from Cairo University, are the other three.

Mrs. Huda Sharawi, on the right, in front of her home after a meeting of the EFU, 1945 (Photograph courtesy of al-Akhbar)

CHAPTER FIVE

The Statist Socialist Phase
(1952–1970s)

This phase of Egyptian feminism began with the Egyptian "revolution" of July 23, 1952, when a clandestine army group—the Free Officers—staged a successful coup d'état and took over the country. This group forced King Faruk, the last ruling member of the Mohammad Ali dynasty, to abdicate and one year later, in June 1953, abolished the monarchy altogether. Egypt began a new chapter in its history. The coup d'état led by Gamal Abdel Nasser gave birth to a new regime that took upon itself the charge of the social reconstruction of Egypt, a charge that was fraught with ambiguities and problems from the outset (Baker 1978).

Egypt's transition from "traditionalism" to "modernity," although begun more than a century earlier, had been frustrated by external and internal factors: a land-scarce economy, a surplus population, a lopsided production structure, substantial unemployment, capital shortage, dependence on the outside world, maldistribution of wealth, and a half-paralyzed bureaucracy (Ibrahim 1982b). The continuing British occupation, coupled with the dislocations occasioned by World War II and the Arab-Israeli conflict resulting from the loss of war in Palestine in 1948, further aggravated these problems, thereby creating a revolutionary situation in Egypt in the middle of the twentieth century (Baker 1978; El-Hamamsy 1975).

During the first years of the revolution, the Free Officers did not seem committed to a fixed ideology or social doctrine. Mostly in their thirties, many had actively participated in political agitation but through such varied and divergent political groups as the communist Young Egypt and the fundamentalist Muslim Brothers. There were those among the officers who held Marxist views and those who held Islamic fundamentalist views, but there were others who fluctuated between ideologies.

As the military leaders of the new regime, the ideology of the Free Officers developed in a gradual and piecemeal fashion that from 1952 to 1970 passed through several distinct phases (Ibrahim 1982b). During the first years of the revolution, the officers devoted their efforts to the consolidation of power and the mobilization of mass support. Seeking discipline and the abolition of political competition, they violently punished manifestations by left and right, purged the army, police, and civil service, and censored the press. Political parties at first were asked to purge themselves of all corrupt elements and then later in 1953 were banned altogether (Dessouki 1978). From then on, a single-party system characterized the regime throughout its duration; the Liberation Rally (1953–1956) was followed by the National Union (1956–1962) and then by the Arab Socialist Union, which remained the only political party in Egypt up to 1977, well into the Sadat regime. In addition to eliminating political competition, the new regime also developed a number of authoritarian features as the government penetrated groups and associations and brought them under its legal and financial control (Dessouki 1978).

From 1956 to 1960, the leaders of "revolution" turned their attention to Egypt's economic problems, and the political revolution of 1952 began to have its counterpart in the economic sphere (Baker 1978:49). With the objective of "social justice," the government implemented a number of state policies "to rectify the injustices of the existing social order." These policies included land reform, progressive taxation, rent controls, nationalization, Egyptianization, minimum and maximum wage limits, subsidies, price controls, and free social services. During the following period, 1960 to 1966 (the socialist transformation phase), the government issued another set of laws that came to be known as the Socialist Laws. These laws included the implementation of the First Five-Year Plan; the expansion of the public sector; further limits on landownership; further cuts on rents; the allocation of 50 percent of seats in all popular elected bodies to workers and peasants; the decreeing that 25 percent of the profits of all companies should go to the workers and employees; and the employment of all university and trade school graduates by the public sector (Ibrahim 1982b). For all intents and purposes, by the mid-1960s the espoused ideology of the new regime was clearly socialist in orientation. Faced with many challenges, the Free Officers had attempted to implement one of the most ambitious programs of political, economic, and social change ever attempted in a noncommunist Third World country.

• WOMEN AND SOCIALISM •

Although a great deal has been written about capitalist versus socialist political structures, very little of it touches on the issue of the role of women in society. Karl Marx in his critique of capitalism does not address himself directly to women because he does not consider them an analytical category of oppression, but rather members of various classes (Boulding 1976:24). Although not an avowed feminist, he also was not antifeminist, but the emancipation of women to him remained a somewhat marginal question. Indeed, he seems to have given it little thought. Engels, who writes more and gives more thought to the issue, sees the emancipation of women as contingent on their emancipation from housework and on their large-scale participation in social production. Yet according to him, this would be achieved only with the abolition of private property and the coming of socialism (Banks 1981).

In the history of Western feminism, socialism as an intellectual tradition seemed the most wholeheartedly feminist. Yet, especially in the United States and England, the relationship between socialism and feminism was by no means smooth or simple. There were many points of contact between the beliefs of the feminists and the feminism of the socialists, grounded as both ideologies were in the doctrine of equality. However, the Marxist doctrine that socialism must come first meant in practice that socialist movements were rarely feminist.

In the socialist movements of the nineteenth century, even socialists who were feminists were unsympathetic to the organized feminist movements because of the limited nature of their goals. Eleanor Marx, the daughter of Karl Marx, argues that "it is with those who would revolutionize society that our work as women lies" (Banks 1981). She expressly repudiates the goals of the feminists by arguing that the improvement in the position of women could come only after the socialist revolution.

Today, socialist societies have a long way to go before women are equal partners to men. The fact that they have a theory that accounts for the possibility of equality and an ideology and policies that support it show up in a variety of practical ways including the fact that women are invariably better represented in the political bodies of socialist countries than they are in nonsocialist countries (Boulding 1976). Whether the quality of male-female relationships is better is another question, as sex stereotyping continues to result in serious inequalities of opportunity for women. This is a fact attested to by the experiences of women in the postrevolutionary Soviet Union, the People's Republic of China, and Cuba.

It is a fundamental concept of Marxism that "human nature" is not an invariable, permanent set of psychosocial characteristics. The psychological characteristics of human beings are rather a product of specific historical circumstances, of a set of production relations, and of class-bound ideologies. The structural changes resulting from the transition to socialism thus are expected to bring about transformations in consciousness, thereby producing "new men" and "new women" (Casal 1979:183). However, the relationship between the structure and superstructure is by no means mechanical, and transformations in the material base do not automatically or instantaneously bring about transformations in consciousness. There is a time lapse between transformations on the structural level and the corresponding changes in the superstructure. Further, superstructural elements are relatively autonomous and often continue to be independently transmitted by socializing agencies such as the family, the schools, and the mass media, despite the fact that changes on the structural level render such elements obsolete or dysfunctional. Transformations in consciousness thus require specific strategies directed at the creation of new values and the initiation of a "revolution" on the cultural level. Even then, such a "revolution" is not always easy.

The Bolshevik Revolution in Russia increased the participation of Russian women in political life. Yet, the female Communists who entered the Communist party before the revolution and became prominent in it afterward for the most part were from the privileged classes and had joined the movement and the party through the agency of male relatives. Although in theory the party accepted women as equal, in practice only those who had a male relative in the party were accepted without objection. Further, these women, either because they avoided theoretical analysis, the area that conferred status within the party, or because they sensed that they would not be welcome in what was almost exclusively a male domain, carried out political tasks rather than engaging in political theorizing. Not one of them ever sat on the Politburo (Farnsworth 1979).

In accordance with Marxist party ideology, which required the subordination of all social causes to the class struggle, Lenin in 1917 had refused separate organizations for women. Later, he was forced to admit that separate organizations for women were a tactical necessity as many Communists, especially men, considered work with women a low priority and "an incidental matter." In 1919, the Zhenotdel, a women's section, which organized all commissions and propaganda teams carrying out women's work, was formed under the jurisdiction of the Central Committee. The Zhenotdel did not grow out of a consensus within the party, but resulted from the persistent and rather unpopular efforts of a small group of female Communists who were committed to the liberation of their own sex and charged with drawing working-class and peasant women into the party. Conservative thinking was surprisingly strong among the masses of Russian women. Change came into their lives only with the frantic drive to industrialization in the First Five-Year Plan and after the enforced political demise of the Zhenotdel in 1930. By 1936, Russian women constituted 40 percent of the labor force. Their growing employment, however, was not a result of the Zhenotdel's efforts on the behalf of women, but was enforced by the needs of the national economy as defined by an authoritarian centralized regime (Farnsworth 1979).

The Chinese Communist revolution was born out of the precepts of Marxism-Leninism, and the Chinese Communist party was formed under

Soviet tutelage in July 1921. Chinese women were even more oppressed than their Soviet sisters, and the first generation of Chinese Communists, like Lenin, had to face a nearly insurmountable problem: How could women become active participants in the revolutionary process when their social conditioning made this a formidable, if not impossible, task? As in the Soviet experience, male cadres shunned assignments to work with women, arguing that "there is little chance for contact between men and women" (Maloney 1979).

In the case of Cuba, the primacy of economic development tasks, which were essential preconditions for the construction of socialism, lay at the root of the revolutionary government's approach to women. The government emphasized the integration of women in the labor force, the development of female resources by means of education, and the mobilization of women to struggle for the general goals of socialist construction but not necessarily for feminist goals (Casal 1979). Postrevolutionary changes in women's status and roles included significant although not radical changes in the level and nature of their employment, and significant changes in the level of their participation in collective activities (other than paid labor) and in mass organizations generally. Changes in legislation emphasized their rights within marriage. There was a marked improvement in their participation in the political system as compared to prerevolutionary levels, although membership in the party and in key party, state, and government structures remained rather low. However, in the ideological realm, changes in the attitudes of both men and women, in the cultural definitions of male and female roles, and in household politics were slower in coming. The ideology of male supremacy embodied in the sexual division of labor still persisted within the family, so that twenty years after the revolution the picture that presented itself was mixed and transitional, with new egalitarian norms coexisting with strong residues of the old sexual ideology and with a generally conservative view of the role of women (Casal 1979).

• EGYPTIAN WOMEN AND THE SOCIALIST EXPERIENCE •

This phase of Egyptian feminism is called "statist" because all the changes that occurred in the status of Egyptian women were initiated by a series of state laws. With the death of Huda Sharawi in 1947, the Egyptian Feminist Union, the only organized activist women's group in Egypt, lost its impetus. It continued to run its dispensaries, schools, and training centers, but its activities were purely welfare activities rather than organized activities aimed at demanding new rights for Egyptian women. The state became the prime feminist as the "woman question" was incorporated into the national strategy for socioeconomic development and became part of state ideology.

Although it is not my concern here to analyze or evaluate the accomplishments of the Nasser regime, the regime's espousal of socialism implied an ideological commitment to equality for women, and the government policy of self-reliance and quick socioeconomic development through rapid industrialization had a direct bearing on the lives and status of Egyptian women. The leaders of the revolutionary government explicitly recognized the problem of female emancipation in the National Charter of 1962 that stated, "Woman must be regarded as equal to man and she must therefore shed the remaining shackles that impede her free movement, so that she may play a constructive and profoundly important part in shaping the life of the country" (quoted from the National Charter).

In accordance with its ambitious plans, the revolutionary government enacted a number of laws designed to ensure the full participation of all able members. Compulsory education for all up to the primary level (six years of schooling) and free education at all levels were envisioned as investments in human resources. Some laws were enacted and designed specifically to help women shed "the remaining shackles" that impeded their free movement; a new constitution and a new labor code gave Egyptian women rights they had never enjoyed previously.

Free and Compulsory Education Laws

A major target of the 1952 revolutionary government was to raise the educational standard of Egyptians. For a long time, there had been a deep concern about the adequacy and efficiency of the educational system, yet the vast majority of the population remained illiterate. According to 1947 census data, 36 percent of males and 16 percent of females were literate, with only a little more than 4 percent of literate males and a little more than 1 percent of literate females holding any kind of certificate (Central Agency for Public Mobilization and Statistics 1972). Article 19 of the 1923 constitution had made primary education a minimum requirement for Egyptian children of both sexes, and in 1933 the Ministry of Education had issued a law making education compulsory for girls and boys between seven and twelve years of age. However, the execution of both the article and the law had been delayed due to the insufficiency of schools (UNESCO 1970).

The aim of the revolutionary government's educational policy was not only to expand educational opportunities, but also to Egyptianize and unify the country's educational system. The education budget was greatly enlarged to make it possible to give every child, whether boy or girl, a free and compulsory minimal education of six years and to make education free in government schools and national universities. After the Tripartite Aggression of 1956, all foreign schools were nationalized and brought under the auspices of the Ministry of Education. The curricula in the three levels of preuniversity education, primary, preparatory, and secondary, were unified, and general examinations decided the transfer of students from one stage to the next. Provisions also were made for adult education, and literacy classes were introduced in factories, schools, barracks, and cultural centers (UNESCO 1970).

Expanding equal educational opportunities for women was not entirely new to Egyptian society, especially among the upper classes. For almost a century, feminists had been clamoring for such opportunities. What the revolution contributed to the education of Egyptian women was changing the concept of the educated woman. The unification of curricula, which aimed to train all Egyptians, whether women or men, for active participation in shaping the life of the country, meant that secondary schools specializing in so-called feminine skills were dropped out of the educational system (UNESCO 1970). Although there were many separate schools for boys and girls, the government emphasized the acceptability of co-education by making all new schools, especially at the primary level, co-educational (Gerner 1984).

Further, the revolutionary government's ideology, which emphasized education and work as legitimate venues for upward social mobility, contributed to making education for women more accepted as a social and economic need and as something of a status symbol. There was an increasing demand for education among the emerging urban middle classes. However, there were several factors operative among the lower classes and in rural areas that continued to favor the education of men over that of women. Thus, in the final analysis, the main beneficiaries of the free and compulsory education laws were upper- and middle-class urban women (Badran 1972)

Traditional views regarding the role of women hindered rural and lower-class urban women from the pursuit of formal education. Even though government schools and institutions of higher education were open to and offered free tuition to both sexes, seeing children through all levels of education remained a costly venture for most parents. Besides needing books, extra clothes, and other materials, students required special attention and a special atmosphere in order to pursue their studies. Further, as students, they for the most part were unproductive and were an economic burden on their families. Especially in rural areas and among the lower classes of urban areas, where sons remained valued over daughters, and in which families had a large number of children and limited income, parents very often gave priority and special attention to the education of their sons, even if their daughters received only primary education or no education at all.

Further, the pursuit of education meant greater freedom for the girls and an opportunity for them to leave home more often. Parents, unwilling to compromise the reputation of their daughters (their greatest asset in the marriage market), preferred the safe way out, which was to keep their daughters under lock and key. As the severe shortage of schools remained a problem in rural areas, this was especially true if the daughters had to travel from their local village to a nearby urban center to attend school. Further still, the absence of domestic help among lower-class families made housework and the care of children the total responsibility of the wife, who to a large extent depended on the assistance of her daughters in the performance of these duties. At the same time, this assistance was vital to the daughters because it provided them with the necessary training for their future roles as housewives and mothers. The completion of even the secondary level of education deprived mothers of this assistance and daughters of their training. It also could mean a postponement of marriage. The high value placed on marrying girls at puberty or upon reaching sixteen (the minimum age limit for marriage set by law) rendered the completion of formal education an insufficiently important reason for a postponement of marriage. These factors also were operative among upper- and middle-class urban families, but to a much lesser degree. Urban areas offered more anonymity and exerted less pressure on families to conform to the traditional values of society.

As a consequence of all these factors, we find that even in 1976, almost six years after the end of the Nasser era, Egyptian women still lagged far behind men in their literacy rates. Although literacy rates had increased for both males and females, there was still much less literacy (22 percent) among females than among males (54 percent). The difference was accentuated in rural areas, where in 1970 only 12 percent of rural women could read or write. Also, the enrollment of boys was greater than that of girls in all levels of education, the difference increasing as one moved up the educational ladder. Thus, in the school year 1969/70, enrollment figures in the primary level, which is compulsory for both sexes, showed a sex ratio of 162:8; at the preparatory level the sex ratio was 213:8, and at the secondary level it was 222:3 (Fergany 1972).

However, compulsory and free education had a positive effect on female education in two ways. First, literacy rates among women in the labor force greatly increased partly because of compulsory education laws but also because of the adult and functional literacy classes introduced in factories and other places of work (Sullivan 1981). In 1974, 46 percent of women in the labor force were literate (Hammam 1980). Second, mainly as an outcome of free education, there was a noteworthy increase in the participation of women in higher education. This, of course, applied to both sexes; thus, while the rate of population increase from 1952 to 1977 was 2.4 percent per year, the rate of increase in university level enrollment was 7.5 percent per year. During the same period, the ratio of male to female students steadily decreased from 13.1:1 to 1.8:1 (El-Guindi 1983). Furthermore, there was a steady increase in the enrollment of women in the practical faculties such as medicine, engineering, veterinary diseases, pharmacy, and dentistry that had been considered exclusively male domains.

Labor Laws

In line with its ideology that "socialism" requires the participation of men and women side by side in the building of the new society, the revolutionary government made conscious efforts to increase the participation of women in the labor force. The labor laws prevalent in the country were not very protective of workers, whether men, women, or children. Workers were not entitled to daily rest periods or a weekly day of rest; they did not receive their wages at regular intervals, and the wages they received often amounted to less than what was stipulated in their contract. Further, they were denied the right to strike or to form trade unions. According to one source, marriage was a sufficient reason for dismissing women from their jobs (Hammam 1980). The 1959 labor code set minimum wages, maximum working hours, and gave workers a share of the profits and the right to form labor associations. The code further stipulated that women be provided with special social services by the employers: seating arrangements where appropriate, exclusion from arduous and night work, two half-hour breaks per day for mothers of infants during the eighteen months following delivery, and fifty-day delivery leaves. The code also stipulated that women could not be dismissed from work as a result of marriage, pregnancy, or delivery and that any establishment with more than one hundred women should provide a day-care center.

One year after the National Charter of 1962, in which the government explicitly recognized the problem of female emancipation, the Ministry of Social Affairs addressed the problem of female labor with a conference on Egyptian working women. The conference report included the ministry's proposal for the encouragement of female labor and the improvement of working conditions based on a survey of the currently employed. Day-care centers, part-time job opportunities, the coordination of husband and wife workplaces, and public education on the important and equal role women could play in the labor force were seen as important programs for broadening female participation. During the 1960s, a plethora of books also appeared on the "woman question," making idealistic assessments of the role of the new socialist woman (Tucker 1976).

Despite these efforts, the overall participation of women in the labor force remained relatively low in comparison to men. The female work participation rate, which was 2.3 percent in 1947, only had increased to 4.8 percent by 1960 (Badran 1972). Further, this rate went up to 6.4 percent in 1961 and remained stable at this rate until 1969 (Fergany 1972). Also, the increase in female labor force participation in urban areas was offset by a corresponding decrease in rural areas. The rise in the educational and vocational standards of women encouraged many of them to join the industrial rather than the agricultural sector. The agricultural sector previously had absorbed a high percentage of female workers mainly because agricultural work does not require special training, education, or qualifications, and a large proportion of the women listed under agriculture did not work for wages but engaged in agricultural activity within the family. After 1952, many women left the agricultural sector to join industry, and the percentage of females working in agriculture as a proportion of the total number of females working declined from 43 percent in 1961 to 26 percent in 1976. At the same time, industry expanded its female labor force from an insignificant 3.3 percent in 1961 to 11.7 percent in 1971 and to 13 percent in 1976 (Sullivan 1981). However, women were concentrated in some industries rather than others.

The most noticeable change in female labor during that period was that the educational level of working women increased and was even higher than the educational level of men. Almost 15 percent of working women held a university degree, and these working women accounted for virtually all growth in female employment. These women came to hold 16.3 percent of the scientific, professional, and technical positions in the country, although they represented only 8.8 percent of the total paid workforce (Gerner 1984). Although teaching and medicine remained the most socially acceptable professions for women, absorbing 90 percent of female professional workers, women joined all professions, except the judiciary, the armed forces, and certain posts in diplomatic corps, in increasing numbers (Abdel Kader 1973).

Although after the nationalizations of the 1960s the state emerged as the major employer in all sectors of the economy, in terms of female employment the private sector, especially in manufacturing, commerce, and services, remained the major employer of women for a number of years (Sullivan 1981). The civil service law itself did not discriminate between men and women in any way. A grade system decided placement and promotion on the basis of education, job performance, and length of service, regardless of sex. In practice, however, there was discrimination. Some ministries, such as foreign affairs, communication, and supplies, employed women in very small numbers. The Ministry of War did not employ any. The law stated that priority for jobs be established solely by performance in a civil service examination, yet some employers were reluctant to hire women, and the Civil Service Central Personnel Office did not try to force women on these employers. On the positive side, we find that in the ministries where women workers were welcome, such as the Ministry of Education (which employed the largest proportion of female workers) and the Ministry of Social Affairs, there was no discrimination in appointment or promotion. During the period, two women in succession were appointed minister of social affairs.

It is a generally accepted economic principle that the participation of women in paid work outside the home increases with economic development. Advances in technology and the introduction of power equipment in plants and factories create new jobs for women (Collver and Langlois 1962; Youssef 1971; Haikal 1971). Some observers feel that this principle needs some modification in describing developing Muslim countries, such as Egypt. In the early 1970s, Nadia Haggag Youssef published her now classic work, *Women and Work in Developing Societies* (1974), in which she forwards her thesis that the social norms of veiling and seclusion of women prevalent in developing Muslim countries have special repercussions on the participation of women in economic activities, especially in the nonagricultural labor force. Her comparison of the female work participation rate in the nonagricultural labor force in developing Muslim countries (including Egypt) and in developing non-Muslim countries shows that there is some basis to her thesis. Muslim women compared to women in other developing countries had the lowest rates of economic participation, particularly in nonagricultural activities.

Economic expansion demanded the assistance of women as well as men and the number of Egyptian women working outside the home continued to increase, but the working woman, especially the married working woman, was not a totally accepted phenomenon. Egyptian working women, like working women all over the world, had to adjust the demands of home life with the exigencies of a career. For the married woman, the problem was especially serious, as there were important adjustments necessary in intrafamilial relations before she could discharge both her family and work duties satisfactorily. A study of ten Egyptian upper-middle-class urban families reveals that in some families in which the wife was working the husband persisted in assuming his traditional role and in demanding from his wife all the services and attentions a nonworking wife would have been able to offer. Although the physical and psychological strain on the wife was sometimes difficult to bear, she condoned her husband's attitudes (Abdel Kader 1971).

The material, social, and psychological conflicts arising from women working both inside and outside the home had their impact on job performance. Employers gave many reasons for their reluctance to hire women. Among the reasons was the greater absenteeism rate among women, higher among married than unmarried ones. Especially in industry, employers complained that they had to employ a larger number of workers to avoid disturbances caused by a high rate of absenteeism among female workers (Badran 1972:18). Employers also complained that women workers reported late to work, left the labor force at a younger age than men, and were reluctant to be geographically mobile. A 1970 study showed that 74 percent of female workers as compared to 55 percent of male workers were concentrated in big cities and that 83 percent of the women refused to work in rural areas even if this implied promotion (Haikal 1971). Although the new labor laws gave female workers many rights, in some instances these laws had adverse effects on female employment. Employers who hired more than one hundred women had to provide day-care centers; thus, women employees cost more than male employees, and to avoid the extra cost, employers made it a point not to employ the one hundredth woman.

There were many attempts to improve working conditions for women. More and more women had come to assume positions of responsibility in trade unions, especially in such industries as petroleum and textiles, and also in banking and commercial establishments. In the 1970s, there were two hundred thousand female labor unionists out of a total labor union population of 1 million. Some female labor unionists struggled to overcome the obstacles and problems facing working women, to secure better terms of employment, and to implement services for working mothers and their families. In fact, labor unions did begin to assume direct responsibility for providing a variety of services for workers and their families by way of supplementing legislation in such areas as medical services (extending them to the families), feeding, transportation, recreational facilities, and the establishment of day-care centers (Abdel Kader 1973:39).

Prior to the 1952 revolution, women's voluntary organizations had started a movement for the establishment of nursery schools or day-care centers for children aged three to six. The movement had started, surprisingly enough, in rural areas, which explains why today there are more rural than urban nursery schools in Egypt. The movement gained momentum after the revolution, but in 1970, although there were 914,850 children between three and six years of age, only 46,998 (5 percent) attended nursery school. Although there were 978 nursery schools operating in Egypt, 63 percent were located in rural areas, 36 percent in urban areas, and the rest in desert areas. It was estimated that Cairo alone needed six hundred new nurseries (*Al-Akhbar,* October 10, 1971).

On the whole, the struggle to improve the working conditions of female workers was concentrated in the industrial and urban areas. Agricultural workers, both male and female, still suffered from underpayment and overwork, but there were no active attempts to improve these conditions and no labor legislation to regulate employment.

Political Rights

Egyptian women gained the right to vote and stand for political office in 1956, when the constitution stated that voting was the right of all Egyptians and that it was their duty to participate in public affairs. This right aroused various reactions, and women's associations were active in stimulating women to register on voting lists. Unfortunately, the majority of Egyptian women did not go to the polls to exercise their newly won rights; only two women candidates were elected to the Egyptian Parliament (El-Hamamsy 1958; Hamza 1970). In the following elections in 1957, five women were elected to the National Assembly, but still the number of women voters was very small—only 144,983 women registered to vote as compared to 5,575,672 men. In 1965, the number of women voters increased to two hundred and fifty thousand, and in 1967 it reached 1 million. However, only 11.5 percent of Egyptian males did not vote in 1967, while 76.7 percent of females failed to exercise their right (Diab 1969:277).

The low rate of participation of women in political affairs was due to many factors. For one, voting for women was not obligatory as it was for men. Also, the belief that politics was an exclusively male domain, the lack of time and interest among women, and the objections of husbands and family kept many women out of the political arena (Badran 1977). There was still a large proportion of citizens of both sexes who objected to women's right to vote. A 1969 study of public opinion in Egypt found that 33 percent of the inhabitants of Cairo believed that women should not have a vote in political affairs because (1) it was against customs, traditions, and religion; (2) women were not equal to men; and (3) women's only responsibility was the home. The same study found that there were more males than females among those who objected to women's participation in politics. It also found that younger, educated, and middle-class individuals were more in favor of women's participation than older, uneducated, lower-class individuals, regardless of sex (Diab 1969:201)

Nevertheless, the Nasser regime was greatly supportive of women's participation in the political life of the country. In the 1971 elections, seven women (out of twenty-eight running) were elected to the Arab Socialist Union, the only political party in the country. A special committee for women was one of the standing committees of the union and operated on various levels. The committee included women members of the National Assembly, representatives from the government, members of unions, professionals, married women, and representatives from family planning units (Badran 1972:31).

Family Planning

One of the most serious problems facing the Nasser regime was the country's population growth rate. Egypt's demographic profile in the 1950s and 1960s showed that it had one of the highest population growth rates in the world. Due to improved medical and health care, the gap between birth rates and death rates had widened, thus producing a population growth rate of 1.96 percent, three times that of Spain and four times that of Britain (Gadalla 1968). This high rate of population growth was from the outset almost an insurmountable obstacle frustrating all development efforts. The National Charter of 1962 clearly stated that "population increase constitutes the most dangerous obstacle that faces the Egyptian people in their drive towards raising the levels of production, in an effective and an efficient way. Attempts at family planning deserve the most sincere efforts" (quoted from the National Charter).

A family planning program was launched in 1966 with the Supreme Council for Family Planning as the national body responsible for family planning services and activities. The council conducted its activities through three thousand health facilities and mother-child health centers scattered throughout the country. Services were almost free to the recipients, and contraceptives (mainly birth control pills and intrauterine devices) were available at nominal prices. The program, which met with least success in the peasant communities, failed to communicate the concept of family planning in its broad sense to the public. In January 1969, the users of family planning services in both the program and the private sector were only 10 percent of the married women between the ages of fifteen and forty-four (Badran 1972). Although the failure of the family planning program was attributed to many factors, the traditional status of Egyptian women was one of the most important of these factors.

As was shown in preceding chapters, the traditional role of Egyptian women in both rural and urban areas was for the most part a domestic one. In a predominantly agrarian society where marriage is considered an economic necessity and children an economic asset and a future security for their parents in old age, children were wanted in large numbers and, hence, a large measure of a woman's status was derived from her childbearing potential (El-Hamamsy 1958). The importance of the procreational function of women in peasant societies was among the factors that confronted the Egyptian family planning program in Egypt.

Another variable related to the status of women and one acknowledged by most writers as a major factor in the population problem was the value of early marriage (Ammar 1954; Ayrout 1963; Shanawany 1968). Religious sanctions encouraged early marriage, and the legal minimum age for marriage was sixteen for girls and eighteen for boys. Polygamy and men's right to divorce at will added greatly to women's insecurity. Some women tried to have as many children as possible in order to make it impossible for the husband to afford a second wife or consider a divorce (El-Hamamsy 1972).

The rise in the educational and economic status of Egyptian women had an influence on family planning. There was evidence that the education of women was negatively correlated with fertility. The relation of women's education to fertility, as taken from the 1960 census, was as follows: Illiterate mothers had an average of 4.05 children per married woman, those with primary education had 3.66, and those with secondary and university education had 1.86 children. The difference was even more significant in a comparative study of couples after a marriage duration of thirty to thirty-five years. The illiterate mothers had an average of 7.11 children, those with primary education, 6.06, and those with secondary and university education, 3.08 children (Shanawany 1968).

The attitudes of educated women toward their role as wives and mothers had a great influence on the number of children they desired to bring into the world. Educated women, especially when gainfully employed, were less insecure about their husbands' right to divorce or marry more than one wife. In fact, the courts showed that a large number of the divorce cases were initiated by educated women against their husbands. As for polygamy, it became nearly nonexistent among the educated classes; according to official statistics, it occurred in only 3 percent of all marriages contracted. There also was evidence that marriage age differed with educational attainment. In a survey of teachers working in Alexandria governorate, the average ideal age of marriage for women was 25.85 years, and there was an inverse relationship observed between educational attainments and stated ideal number of children (Kamel et al. 1970:17–36).

Although there was no conclusive evidence that the recruitment of women into work outside the home was a deterrent to fertility, it was enough to know that working women had fewer children. In the late 1960s, the chairperson of the Family Planning Board, Aziz Bindary, attempted to put the relationship between work outside the home and low fertility to a practical test by advocating the establishment of a number of small factories or workshops where women could find employment. Bindary insisted that education and the introduction of contraceptives were insufficient by themselves as they had failed to bring about the necessary check on the population explosion. The kernel of his argument was that it was no use providing women with education unless they also were provided with jobs. Such jobs must take women out of their houses and out of the area of male dominance. Besides small factories or workshops that would employ only women, he also advocated that women be employed in far greater numbers in the service and maintenance industries (Abdel Kader 1973:59). The experiment was implemented on a very small scale and for bureaucratic reasons was latter discontinued. The majority of Egyptian women remained illiterate and unemployed outside the home.

Family planning was not an important issue in the other phases of the Egyptian feminist movement. The main thrust to the call for the emancipation of Egyptian women that started at the turn of the century was in education, work, and suffrage issues. This was especially true because raising the fertility issue at an earlier date would have met with great resistance. Nevertheless, the efforts of Egyptian feminists were bound to be of major assistance to the family planning program, a fact evidenced by the role played by women's voluntary organizations in this area.

By 1970, there were 4,992 women's voluntary organizations (1,299 located in Cairo) working in the social welfare field. In general, these had developed on an individualistic basis, and although most were limited to women, some included men and women. The need for the coordination of the activities of these organizations led to the establishment of the Egyptian Union of Organizations (Badran 1972). Under the sponsorship of the Ministry of Social Affairs and guided by the coordinating efforts of the Egyptian Family Planning Association, many of these voluntary organizations played a major role in the family planning program. In 1970, there were 392 family planning centers run by these voluntary organizations, 232 in urban areas, 157 in rural areas, and 3 in desert areas (Abdel Kader 1973:60-61).

Although the contribution of these centers to fertility control was limited, they contributed greatly to the health and well-being of many women, a vast majority of whom admitted that they had resorted to illegally induced abortions at least once. These voluntary family planning centers also led to the recognition and encouragement of the role of women volunteers in the family planning program (Abdel Kader 1973: 61).

CHAPTER SIX

The *Infitah* Phase (1970s–Present)

The Sadat era began with the sudden death of Nasser on the afternoon of September 30, 1970, while he was at the Cairo International Airport bidding farewell to a number of Arab leaders. These leaders were leaving Egypt at the termination of a summit meeting that had been convened to settle differences that had led to the bloody Black September confrontation between the King Hussein regime and the Palestinians. Anwar Sadat, Egypt's vice-president, succeeded to the presidency after overcoming serious opposition from a number of quarters. Although at first Sadat followed in Nasser's footsteps, claiming repeatedly that his regime was a continuation of Nasser's, after the 1973 October War, Sadat began to rule in his own right. After 1973, there was an almost one-hundred-eighty-degree turn in the country's economic and political ideology as Sadat's open-door economic policy came to replace Nasser's welfare socialism.

• EGYPT'S *INFITAH* •

In opting to follow a course diametrically opposed to that of his predecessor, Sadat was by no means behaving in a unique or unusual manner. "Swings" from closed- to open-door economic policies have been quite common in the postcolonial history of many countries of the Third World. An open-door economic policy (ODEP) exists when a ruling party sanctions transfers of capital, technology, and labor from foreign sources into the nation (Kennedy 1981). Adopting such a policy decision may be internally or externally influenced or may be a combination of both. Whatever the case, who opens the door, how far, what flows through it, from what directions, and in what quantities are vital questions. Yet, the economic doors of Third

World countries are rarely really closed so that closed- and open-door economic policies are no more than analytically ideal types. In shifting from closed- to open-door economic policies, Egypt was merely restructuring its international economic relations, shifting "openness" from one geopolitical direction—the Eastern Bloc—to another—the northwest (Abdel Khaleq 1981).

The reversal of Egypt's socialist, closed-door planned economic policy in favor of an economy open to market forces and private initiative received official endorsement when Sadat declared in his 1974 October Paper that *infitah* would "free the country from the economic restrictions that had bound it for so long." Most interpretations of Egypt's reversal to ODEP emphasize either Sadat's personal orientation as a pro-Western politician who stood for free enterprise and a capitalist economy or the growth of new social forces whose interests were best served by ODEP (Dessouki 1981). Yet, the reversal, which was in the making for some time, was the natural outcome of the convergence of a number of internal and external forces. The roots of the reversal were to be found in the country's abortive attempts to achieve socialism in the 1960s, but international organizations and foreign governments were not less influential in charting Egypt's course in its transition to *infitah* (Dessouki 1981; Abdel Khaleq 1981).

Of the internal factors, Egypt's defeat in the 1967 Arab-Israeli war, the drain of the Yemen war, and the termination of U.S. economic aid, among other things, had a profound effect in slowing down Egypt's socioeconomic growth. The loss of Suez Canal revenues and the Sinai oil fields, the massive destruction of the Suez Canal cities, and the massive displacement of nearly 1 million people from those cities added to the strain on the country's economy, thereby bringing about a sharp decline in its investments in socioeconomic development. Egypt's rate of growth for that period was no more than 1 percent annually (Ibrahim 1982b).

The rise in the volume of Egypt's imports, particularly consumer goods, without a comparable rise in the volume of its exports resulted in an increase in its balance-of-payments deficit. Under these conditions, Egypt came under considerable external pressure to "redefine its national priorities." Early in 1974, the World Bank dispatched one of its advisers to Egypt to recommend a development strategy that would "permit making better use of Egyptian ingenuity and enterprise, encourage private savings and the repatriation of capital from abroad, help the export effort, and allow for domestic competition between private and public firms" (Balassa 1977:87–97). However, the most obvious external pressure came from the International Monetary Fund (IMF) and the Consultative Group. The IMF made the extension of any further credit contingent upon the implementation of a set of measures that would restructure Egypt's internal economy. These measures in effect forced the Egyptian economy to open its doors to foreign goods. The Consultative Group (an association of all countries and regional and international organizations providing aid to Egypt) prescribed a development formula for Egypt that called for the amendment of laws to give more incentive to the private sector, end the monopoly of foreign trade by the public sector, and minimize administrative obstacles confronting foreign investors (Abdel Khaleq 1981; Dessouki 1981).

In response to these pressures, between 1974 and 1977 a number of new economic laws were enacted that amounted to a reversal of Egypt's socialist transformation, tilting it progressively toward a capitalist laissez-faire, laissez-passez economic policy. By 1978, the number of foreign commercial agencies investing in Egypt had exceeded one thousand and represented two thousand six hundred firms from fifty-six countries. Among these firms, multinationals from West Germany, Britain, France, Italy, Switzerland, and the United States topped the list (Shouaib 1979). Thus, neither Egypt nor Sadat really opted for *infitah*. The policy was imposed by the convergence of both internal and external factors. Further, Egypt under *infitah* did not simply look outside but was forced to turn northwest, so that by 1978, Egypt was firmly integrated within the web of world capitalism.

According to official and semipopular views, Egypt's new economic policy was to be a real panacea (Abdel Khaleq 1981). The full weight of orthodox economic analysis was brought to bear in support of propositions that free trade and free capital flow would solve all the country's economic problems. *Infitah*, coupled with Sadat's foreign policy, would bring peace, reconstruction, and prosperity for all. Indeed, there was no reason to believe that a liberal economic policy would not be associated with high rates of economic growth. Countries, especially those of Latin America, that had adopted such a policy during the past twenty years had achieved such high rates of growth that their experiences had been described as no less than "economic miracles."

Unfortunately, such high rates of growth had not brought prosperity to all. As the president of Brazil once eloquently expressed it, "Brazil is doing well, but the people are not" (Amin 1981). Satisfying the basic needs of the lower-income group of any country is less dependent on the rate than on the pattern of growth. At least in the initial stages of their implementation, open-door development strategies have been known to exacerbate internal inequities between the rich and poor and in some instances to worsen the level of absolute poverty. In the absence of specific strategies to ensure that the basic needs of people in the lower-income brackets are met, the poor usually accrue little benefits from the "economic miracles" of "open-door" economic policies (Amin 1981).

After *infitah,* the change in the nature of Egypt's economic activities was coupled with a net decrease in employment opportunities. Indeed, there was a striking difference between the rate of growth of employment during the years of the closed door and during the period of greater liberalization. For the latter period (1970 and beyond), total employment increased at less than half the rate achieved during the years 1959 to 1965 (Amin 1981). The increase in foreign investment meant that a significant portion of domestic savings and skills was diverted from labor-intensive production toward those branches of production that were either part of or in the service of the foreign sector. In consequence, the primary and tertiary sectors expanded at the expense of the secondary (manufacturing and agriculture) (Abdel Khaleq 1981). The share of manufacturing (and related activities) in the labor force, which had increased from 8 percent in 1947 to 13 percent in 1966, declined to 12.4 percent in 1971 and 12.6 percent in 1976 (Ibrahim 1982b). The opening of the country's economic doors also involved a "secondary transfer" of labor from agricultural production to imported enterprises subsidiary to multinational corporations; thus, agriculture's share of the labor force substantially and steadily declined (Hopkins 1981). Increased rural unemployment and decreased subsidies for agriculture further increased the rural-urban income gap (Korayem 1981).

In the major cities, social disparities widened and class lines hardened as engaging in private-enterprise business activities became the main channel for upward social mobility. As the doors of employment closed within Egypt, skyrocketing oil prices after the 1973 October War opened them in other parts of the Arab world. Working in the oil-rich Arab countries, mainly Saudi Arabia, Libya, and Kuwait, became the only means of survival for many lower- and middle-class Egyptian peasants, laborers, and professionals. By 1980, the astronomical increase in the number of Egyptians working abroad had made Egypt one of the major labor-exporting countries in the region (Ibrahim 1982a).

With the reversal of Egypt's economic policies, the Egyptian political system underwent fundamental transformation. Within a relatively short period, *infitah* had created a new class consisting mainly of business entrepreneurs. Some members of this new class belonged to the prerevolutionary upper and upper-middle classes that had been suppressed after the 1952 revolution but that had resurfaced after economic liberalization. Others, however, were nouveaux riches, who through their business dealings and quick profit had come to constitute a stratum of new millionaires (Hinnebusch 1981; Ibrahim 1982b). With a vested interest in the continuation of *infitah,* the members of this new class sought ways and means to gain greater access to political decisionmaking in the country.

Nasser's authoritarian yet "populist-nationalist" regime had resulted from a "breakthrough" for the emerging middle classes into a political arena heretofore dominated by the national upper classes. The Nasser regime had seen its main task as the redistribution of power and wealth from the upper to the middle and lower classes. Although real political power remained concentrated in the hands of a charismatic leader and a military cadre trying to impose a revolution from above, the welfare dimension of the regime had secured for it a minimum of passive, but broad, middle- and lower-class popular support (Baker 1981; Hinnebusch 1981). Sadat, by contrast, in seeking legitimacy among the new and expanding bourgeoisie and as a strategy to institutionalize his control experimented with a "multiparty" system. He hoped that in return for greater political freedom, the new elite would refrain from challenging his authority as president and would refrain from mass mobilization. However, as the new elites were not content with nominal participation and did try to mobilize mass support in a challenge of his regime, he was forced to curb the experiment. The resulting system was a kind of uninstitutionalized limited elite pluralism that opened up greater informal access for the bourgeoisie but denied access to leaders who would mobilize and speak for the masses. This system clearly favored the haves over the have-nots (Hinnebusch 1981).

By 1977, *infitah* was producing a broad, if still inchoate, domestic opposition that gathered together elements from a wide spectrum of opinion and that diminished Sadat's ability to carry the country with him in his economic and foreign policy reorientations (Baker 1981). There was ample evidence of fragmentation within the elite and lack of consensus on the contents, goals, and means of *infitah*. Ministers quarreled in public, and there was a high turnover of senior economic advisers (Dessouki 1981). There also was ample evidence of rising dissatisfaction among the masses as the much talked about "prosperity" appeared to be far from forthcoming. Instead, there was flagrant evidence of widening class gaps, a dismantling of Egypt's welfare dimension, and new forms of repression. The opening of the country's doors to Western multinationals and imports had had drastic effects on the prices and availability of necessary goods and had flooded the markets with an assortment of high-priced, sometimes unnecessary, Western consumer goods that were far beyond the means of the majority of the masses. A good part of popular discontent arose from the sense that the economic burdens of the times were being shared more unequally than ever. The escalating privileges of the new ODEP class were emphasizing class differences more than ever before. In Cairo and the large cities, fleets of high-priced limousines, luxury buses for tourists, luxury apartments, and hotel construction grated on a consciousness rubbed raw by fears of further price rises and subsidy reductions. When the subsidy reductions did indeed come in response to pressures from the IMF, large-scale demonstrations rocked the country's key cities, leaving an estimated seventy-nine killed, one thousand wounded, and some one thousand two hundred and fifty jailed. The Egyptian army, with its tanks and officers, flooded the streets of Cairo for the first time in more than thirty years.

Egypt's *infitah,* intended as economic policy, had its consequences on the cultural and sociomoral level. As doors were opened for economic activity, there was a simultaneous movement of people—foreigners in for investment, Egyptians out for labor—and with it new exposures. Along with consumer goods there also was importation of ideas (El-Guindi 1981). As foreign goods and foreign capital stood at the door, a sufficiently large class of consumers with sufficiently high incomes had to be ready to receive these goods. Just as factors of production and purchasing power had to be diverted from domestic products toward foreign goods, so, too, national culture had to give way to an interest in the culture from which these goods originated. In a word, "economic liberalization" also meant "Westernization" and the submerging of Egyptian culture (Amin 1981). At the same time, the rapid increase of money-wealth for Egyptian returnees from oil-rich countries led these Egyptians to develop new consumption patterns made all the easier by earlier deprivation and by the endless demonstration of luxury goods in the local markets. Such consumption patterns set in motion a demonstration effect, so that even those who could not consume at the same level but who belonged to the same reference group began to crave luxury goods and to seek quick means of obtaining them (Ibrahim 1982a). Just as the alienation from national culture had devalued authenticity, the new materialism undermined ethics. In a word, *infitah* seemed to go hand in hand with *inhilal,* that is, "societal disintegration" (El-Guindi 1981).

Westernization was confined to the upper classes. Paradoxically, and as happened before, the increased Westernization of the upper classes was paralleled by increased ethnocentrism, xenophobia, and fanaticism among the middle and lower classes. As the open door magnified Western presence, Islam and Islamic symbols came to safeguard national identity and culture. Among the sociopolitical forces that surfaced in Egypt after *infitah* were fundamentalist Islamic groups. Historically, militant Islamic groups were grass-roots movements with an appeal mainly to the lower-middle class. The 1952 revolution had temporarily pulled the rug out from under these groups by appealing to lower and middle classes and appropriating the support of most of their constituency. For a while, secular ideology ruled supreme. Yet the 1967 defeat of Egypt at the hands of Israel dealt a serious blow to the Nasser regime. Faith in Nasser and his secular ideology, which until the defeat had been unshakable, was replaced by doubt and loss of security and self-esteem. As usually happens in times of crisis, a climate of intense and visible religiousness emerged. It was in this mood that Islamic groups began to win back the support of increasing segments of Egypt's middle classes. Yet what started as a diffuse religiousness in the late 1960s developed into organized militancy in the 1970s after the reversal of Egypt's economic policies and the mounting troubles of *infitah*.

For a period of thirty years, Egypt had experimented with the two most forceful models of development—the nationalist-socialist model (1952–1970) and the liberal capitalist model (1970–1980). Neither of the two experiments had been allowed to run its natural course, but also neither had fulfilled its promises. The failure of the second experiment forced a serious reexamination of secular ideology and morality. In the absence of credible secular national visions and effective programs of action to enhance the present and future socioeconomic prospects of the middle and lower classes, Islam and Islamic traditions presented themselves as the only viable alternatives, and the appeal of Islamic militancy grew until it became a tidal wave (Ibrahim 1980).

• WOMEN AND ODEPS •

Women constitute the majority of the poor, underemployed, and socially and economically disadvantaged in most societies. ODEPs that are generally disadvantageous to the poor of Third World countries are especially so for women (Sen 1985). As was evident in the previous chapter, traditional thinking subordinates women to positions of inferiority, limits their roles to childbearing, childrearing, and housework, and usually proves remarkably stubborn to break down. Yet, socialist societies with their planned strategies for satisfying basic human needs improve women's overall condition by giving them more rights and education through greater employment in the nontraditional labor force. By contrast, the reshuffling of the production structure to fulfill the needs of an economy open to uncontrolled market forces and the free flow of foreign capital and imports reinforce and even exacerbate the subordination of women by reducing their employment opportunities and increasing the levels of their absolute and relative poverty.

In terms of the sectoral effects of the reorientation of production structure, women lose employment opportunities in agriculture and industry. In rural areas, women's access to land, labor, technology, credit, and other inputs into cultivation worsens or at best does not improve. Mechanization and the introduction of cash crops improve the economic position of men but drastically reduce employment and income for women, even in the same household.

In the industrial sector, the picture is more mixed. On the whole, with the suppressing of manufacture, women's participation in the industrial labor force decreases. However, while women's employment in traditional crafts, which are themselves dying, decreases, women's employment in certain export-based industries increases. Yet, within these industries, women are segregated into a narrow range of occupations, their wages are low, and their employment is short term, with a high turnover. Once women lose their jobs, they are left no choice but to move into the so-called informal sector. Even there they occupy the lower end of the "informal" spectrum and have little chance of moving out. Not only do they come to constitute a larger share relative to men of this sector, but women's activities in this sector come to constitute the largest proportion of total female employment.

As women lose employment opportunities in agriculture and industry, some of them, but in disproportionate numbers, find employment in the tertiary sectors (services and commerce). As the number of private business firms increases, the demand for highly skilled, bi- or even tri-lingual secretaries increases. Some women may even start their own businesses. However, because of the skills, education, and capital required of such enterprises, employment opportunities are limited to a very small stratum of women.

Yet, more important than the growth of female poverty under ODEPs is the growth of reactionary tendencies and impulses that further subdue women and force a "retraditionalization" of their roles. The subordination of women and restrictions on their activity and mobility are embedded in most traditional cultures. Defined by cultural norms and reinforced by myths, proverbs, educational systems, and the mass media, such attitudes are deeply ingrained in the consciousness of both men and women. The call to cultural purity for women means attacks on their civil status, physical mobility, and work outside the home. Yet, traditional religion remains the most powerful social force circumscribing and delineating their lives. As women become pawns in the struggle between the forces of "tradition" and so-called modernity, fundamentalist religion often is used as a tool to return women to their "proper" place within the home, in the family, and in society at large.

• EGYPTIAN WOMEN AND *INFITAH* •

Egypt's *infitah* has affected the lives of Egyptian women in a number of ways.

Employment Opportunities for Egyptian Women Under *Infitah*

As noted earlier, ODEPs have a tendency to decrease employment opportunities for women in the agricultural sector and increase their work load. With the suppression of local industry, crafts, and artisan production, women also lose employment opportunities in the manufacturing sector of the economy. For the majority of poor, mostly unskilled women, this means resorting to the low-paying, seasonal, and sporadic employment of the informal sector, of which they come to constitute the bulk and which once they join have little chance of leaving. For their more skilled, better educated, but numerically insignificant upper-class sisters, the picture is somewhat brighter. For them, ODEP creates greater demand and better employment opportunities in the form of relatively well-paying, if mostly secretarial and clerical, jobs in the mushrooming private enterprise and multinational firms. With a few deviations imposed by the idiosyncrasies of *infitah* in Egypt, notably the concomitant opening up of employment opportunities in oil-rich countries, this employment pattern has been replicated in Egypt.

As elsewhere, official labor statistics in Egypt obfuscate the real contributions of Egyptian women to the economy. This is so because a significant portion of their work is still unremunerated and also because the Ministry of Manpower does not collect information on the "informal sector" where many women work. The unreliability of statistical data is even more true for the period of *infitah*, partly because of the paucity of new data and partly because the pace of socioeconomic change has been so fast that even so-called "hard data," if available, are outdated before publication (Sullivan 1981). The data for the last census of Egypt was collected in 1974 and published in 1976, only two years after *infitah* was inaugurated officially. Data for a new general census currently are being collected (December 1986), and even preliminary results are not likely to be available for at least two years. In the absence of hard scientific data on the impact of *infitah* on women, this assessment is based on whatever aggregate statistics are available and on the impressionistic rather than empirical observations of scholars in the field.

Even according to statistics published by the Central Agency for Public Mobilization and Statistics (1976), the percentages of women working in agriculture and manufacturing as a proportion of the total number of females working had declined significantly by 1976. Up to the early 1960s, agriculture was the major employer of women; in 1961, it accounted for 43 percent of all female employment. This percentage decreased to 26 percent in 1971 and then to 22 percent in 1976. This decrease was attributable to the increasing value placed on education and to the general shift in the economy from agriculture to nonagricultural pursuits, mainly industry. Both trends, of course, had been set in motion by the socialist, self-reliant economic policy of the Nasser regime, which had directed resources to massive education and to the creation of an industrial base in Egypt. Between the early and middle 1960s, the decrease in the percentage of women working in agriculture had been counterbalanced by an increase in the percentage working in technical and professional occupations as well as an increase in the percentage working in industry. Between 1961 and 1976, the proportion of women working in technical and professional occupations more than tripled, increasing from 8.3 percent of the total in 1961 to 19.3 percent in 1971 and to roughly 26 percent in 1976. Yet, for the same period, the major employer of women in both the public and private sectors was manufacturing; both sectors together accounted for more than half of all female employment.

The decline of manufacturing by 1976 as the major employer of women was matched by an increase in female employment in the banking and service sectors, the latter coming to account for almost 60 percent of all female employment (Sullivan 1981). Immediately after *infitah,* a number of multinational firms began to do business in Cairo, and a number of joint ventures involving Egyptian and foreign partners were formed. At least fifty international banks, forced to flee the country after the massive nationalization of the late 1950s, reopened branches in the major cities. The tourist industry also boomed. Particularly in urban areas, many relatively well-paying jobs, most of them usually defined as women's work (secretaries, bank clerks, tourist guides, and waitresses), were created (Sullivan 1981).

Whatever else the impact of *infitah* on the Egyptian economy, *infitah's* short-term economic impact was beneficial for the women who qualified to occupy these jobs (Sullivan 1981). This was especially true as the earnings from these jobs were significantly higher than the traditionally higher status, but lower-paying jobs still sought by Egyptian men. A waitress in a luxury hotel could earn considerably more than her husband or her father, even though either might be a senior official in a government ministry.

Although according to official figures in 1976 only 1.7 percent of the female labor force occupied executive, administrative, or managerial jobs, Egyptians witnessed a new phenomenon—the emergence of women as top "businessmen" in Egypt's increasingly exciting, dangerous, frustrating, and exhilarating "private sector" (Sullivan 1986). To calm nervous employees and facilitate initial contacts with customers and bankers, some of these women were forced to use "front men" to make it appear as if men were in charge. But these firms in fact were owned and managed by women. Most firms owned by women invested in the service sector (public relations, advertising, marketing, restaurants, tourism, beauty parlors, and health), but some also invested in construction and industry (Sullivan 1986).

Yet, with few exceptions, almost all these women came from the Westernized upper classes. In attempting to draw a profile of Egypt's new class of businesswomen, Earl Sullivan (1986) writes:

> The families into which today's female entrepreneurial elite were born were almost all upper-class and urban. Most come from Muslim families, but one was raised as a Jew and three were Christian. Regardless of religion, however, all the families were Westernized to a considerable degree. . . . The old adage that it takes money to make money is true in the case of all but one of these women. However, very few are in businesses which acquired start-up capital. The way in which wealth helped them most was probably that it provided a substantially different kind of early life from that experienced by most Egyptian men or women (pp. 134–135).

However high their earnings, women working as secretaries in foreign companies, as bank clerks in international banks, as tourist guides, as high-class waitresses in hotels, and especially as top-notch entrepreneurs represent a thin stratum of Egyptian women.

For economic development to be truly liberating for women, it has to propel large numbers of them into the wage labor force (Tucker 1976). The revolutionary reform of the 1950s launched quantitative and qualitative change in education and employment for women. Yet, *infitah* propelled large numbers of women into the informal sector, where they continue to be disenfranchised and where standard statistical measures fail to reflect the complex realities of women's contributions to the labor force. Official labor statistics, which enumerate mainly formal, full-time employment, present a profile of Egyptian society in which a little more than 50 percent of all males above age twelve are economically active and less then 10 percent of all females are economically active. Yet, the growing visibility of the "informal sector" in Egyptian cities and the concomitant growth of poverty and slum areas in these cities are forcing economists and planners to focus their attention on the underemployment, subemployment, and unemployment problems this sector is creating and to seek more accurate and detailed measures of the work roles of its members. Informal observation and experience from other countries indicate that these measures, once developed, are likely to reveal that Egyptian women today constitute a large proportion of this sector.

Migration of Egyptians to Oil-Rich Countries

Although not directly related to *infitah,* large numbers of Egyptians, often with government encouragement, seek employment outside Egypt, especially in oil-rich Arab countries. In the 1950s and early 1960s, most Egyptians working in these countries were professionals (doctors, teachers, engineers), whose numbers never exceeded a few thousand and who came mostly from Egypt's middle classes. The expansion of economic activities in oil-rich countries following the oil-price boom created increasing demands for labor in myriad occupations. Egypt, with its overpopulation, poverty, tremendous capacity to absorb capital, and very well-developed labor and social institutions, became a major labor exporter. By 1980, it was estimated that between 1.5 and 2 million Egyptians were working in these countries, including professionals as well as skilled, semiskilled, and unskilled manual workers. Thus, Egyptian migrants were heavily represented in both the top and low levels of labor power in Arab labor migration (Ibrahim 1981a). Besides being astronomically higher in numbers than their counterparts of the 1950s and 1960s, Egyptian migrants of the 1970s came from a much wider and more varied social base. Even the Egyptian fellah, well known for his deep, almost obsessive attachment to his ancestral land and to his conservative religious village culture, joined the "oil rush" and the massive, almost hysterical out-migration in search of oil money as a means to attain a different and better standard of living. Given Egyptian history, such a development was no less than revolutionary. Rural unemployment was, of course, a strong impetus, but no less important in "raising expectations" among Egyptian fellahin were accounts from urbanites and images of "modern living" projected by the mass media.

On face value, this out-migratory trend was generally beneficial for Egyptian women. For one, the temporary migration of Egyptian males meant that many of the jobs vacated by them were now occupied by women. This was true for both the rural and urban economy and for low and high levels of employment. Regardless of what official statistics said about declining rural employment for women, in some areas of rural Egypt and at certain times of the year, most, in fact virtually all, of the manual workers in the fields were female. For example, in the Nile Delta, between Tanta and Alexandria, women between the ages of fifteen and twenty-five harvested citrus fruit, a job that less than a decade earlier had been done exclusively by males (Sullivan 1981). Given the shortage of agricultural workers generally, women's earnings (reaching five and at times even six and seven Egyptian pounds a day) were exorbitant compared to what such workers normally earned. The absence of men also meant that women in the civil service had better chances of promotion and thus came to be better represented in the higher echelons of government jobs. An informal survey published in one of Egypt's dailies predicted that should the absence of men continue, more women than men would be working in the near future as directors, managers, and administrative executives. Together with vertical mobility there was also horizontal mobility for working women, some of whom even joined the armed forces where they performed clerical duties formerly done by men (Sullivan 1981).

Second, when Egyptian male villagers emigrated, they usually did so without their families. A large number emigrated illegally, with neither official work contracts nor legal residence permits in the countries of employment, so that it was much easier for such men to emigrate alone. Yet, even for "legal" migrants, living in the host countries was much more expensive than living at home, and work contracts rarely provided for residence or travel expenses. So to enhance their savings, especially if they owned land or livestock or had school-age children, Egyptian village migrants usually left their families behind. According to some studies, few as they are, this arrangement was nothing less than "emancipating" for the left-behind wives, whose roles underwent considerable change.

Although responsibilities of these women increased, as did the work load, they acquired new powers, greater chances for self-assertion, and a greater share in decisionmaking (Khafaga 1984). Inside the household, in addition to an already heavy work load, women came to assume the responsibility for managing finances, including the remittances sent by their husbands. In the absence of their husbands, women also came to play a more disciplinary and less protective and affectionate role in the upbringing of their children. Further, women also took over the responsibility of caring for livestock and whatever land the family owned. Outside the household, the absence of the husbands meant that women had to learn to deal with a whole set of new individuals, such as hired workers and merchants, and a set of new institutions, such as agricultural and consumer cooperatives, village banks, and their children's schools. Although due to the male bias, women's participation in formal decisionmaking structures, village popular councils, political parties, committees, and community associations remained minimal, on an individual and informal level, women were able to make major decisions affecting their own and their children's lives and household affairs. Exposure to these institutions even had made some women openly critical of these institutions, and as women gained in confidence, they came to identify themselves more with the community at large rather than with their individual families. On the whole, these women came to taste freedom and sense an independence they had not known formerly (Khafaga 1984).

In addition to this "when-the-cat's-away, the-mice-will-play" style of liberation experienced by some peasant women, the migratory trend was beneficial to Egyptian women in still another unprecedented way. An increasing number of unaccompanied Egyptian women migrated to oil-rich Arab countries. As demand for female teachers in girls schools was high in the sex-segregated educational institutions of these countries, and as such teachers were abundant and underpaid in Egypt, a large percentage were able to secure lucrative long-term contracts. The National Center for Criminological and Sociological Research (1980) estimated that more than one-third of Egyptian migrants were female. Although some worked as domestic servants (nannies and maids), the majority were professional and subprofessional white-collar workers (Ibrahim 1982a). In most cases, the women were single, but even married women sometimes migrated, accompanied by their husbands. The latter situation was dictated by the same factors that led husbands to migrate alone.

On the face of it, it would seem that Egyptian women had everything to gain and nothing to lose by the opening up of work opportunities in oil-rich countries. After all, women were separating from their families of orientation and procreation and were on their own in foreign countries making money. At home, women were enjoying greater vertical and horizontal job mobility. Peasant women, who had long been the traditional "beasts of burden" and the bearers of the brunt of conservatism and sexual subordination, were breaking new grounds in self-assertion. It is easy to herald such developments as new steps in the emancipation of Egyptian women. Yet, for several reasons, a closer look colors this rosy picture with darker hues.

First, there is an inverse relationship between social class origin and conservatism—the higher the class, the less the conservatism. This is so for several reasons, not the least important of which is economic independence, which decreases pressures for conformity and increases the chances of exposure to other cultures and to alternatives to existing codes of conduct and morality. Second, there also is an inverse relationship between the pace of change and misery—the quicker the change and the more sudden it is, the higher the degree of social disintegration, turmoil, and unrest. Certainly, few of Egypt's already Westernized and modernized upper classes resorted to migration to the oil-rich countries to improve their economic status. If they migrated at all, it was to the industrialized countries of the First World such as Europe and the United States. The bulk of Egypt's migrants to oil-rich countries came from the urban middle and lower classes and from rural areas. Normally confined to strictly defined and tenaciously upheld codes of conduct, these migrants were forced to cope with sudden change that challenged many of their deeply held values. Of these values, the subordination of women was the one value most seriously challenged by the structural changes that occurred within the Egyptian family as a result of the opening up of job opportunities in the oil-rich countries.

Insufficient systematic research has been done on the microlevel, socioeconomic impact of this massive migration of Egyptians to oil-rich countries, so that it is impossible to gauge scientifically and empirically its short- or long-run repercussions. However, informal observation indicates that a whole new generation of Egyptian youngsters grew up in single-parent families, with the other parent only a periodic visitor. Although it is hard at present to label the effects of this as positive or negative, it is generally accepted that healthy socialization requires the love and care of both parents. There also was increasing evidence of serious marital discord. Role-reversal was hard to take for husbands whose wives emigrated to hold high-paying jobs, leaving the men behind to care for children and keep house. The situation was even harder for those husbands whose wives secured contracts in countries such as Saudi Arabia that required all employed females to be accompanied by a *mahram*—a husband or an older male relative. In such cases, and especially if the wife's salary exceeded the couple's combined income in Egypt, husbands would accompany their wives even though the men did not have jobs in the host countries. The boredom of staying at home while wives went out to work and the feeling of worthlessness were quite emasculating for many husbands (Ibrahim 1982a).

Informal observation also indicates that there was an increase in the incidents of divorce and polygamy. Husbands, emigrating alone and making more money than ever before, or alone at home receiving their wives' remittances, take on second wives, keeping the fact from their first wives or divorcing them. Single women who "have it made" either at home or abroad face difficulties finding suitable husbands. To avoid loneliness and the stigma of being "old maids," these women sometimes marry much younger but poorer husbands who more often than not propose for financial reasons. After depriving their wives of their life's savings, these men may divorce and marry younger women. This "breakdown" of the traditional Egyptian family seems to many a symbol of insidious materialism and the decadent vulgarization of Egyptian society by oil money.

The Resurgence of Islamic Fundamentalism

Events of the late 1960s and the 1970s in Egypt triggered a revival of religious fervor and a resurfacing of fundamentalist Islamic groups as a militant and powerful sociopolitical force. Although there remains considerable disagreement as to the true causes for this development, when exactly it started, and when it gained momentum, the most visible manifestation in the 1970s of this resurgence was the appearance of increasing numbers of veiled or semiveiled women in the streets and public places of the major cities. What began as scattered acts by a few college women from the urban middle classes soon evolved into a full-fledged, broad-based movement that cut across classes, strata, institutions, and ages. To outside observers familiar with Egypt and especially cosmopolitan Cairo, this movement, which continues unabetted to this day, seemed bizarre and difficult to comprehend.

The initial reactions were deep confusion and astonished bewilderment. Minds brainstormed and introspected, pens wrote and presses churned out newspaper articles, books and pamphlets were published in an attempt to explain away a development that initial reactions depicted as absurd and incongruent. To the progressive and secular-minded, the trend was a regressive development and a retrograde step for the whole of Egypt. Feminists, in particular, were alarmed by what they looked upon as a serious and cruel setback to their long and arduous struggle to "liberate" Egyptian women. It seemed quite ironic that the veil that Egypt's feminist mothers—Huda Sharawi and her followers—had boldly, defiantly, and publicly discarded as a symbol of oppression was being voluntarily reinstituted by the very women feminists had purported to represent. In the midst of bewildered speculation, many questions leaped to the fore: Was the return to the veil an identity crisis, misguided leisure, a fad, a youth protest, an ideological vacuum, individual psychic disturbances, life-crises, social dislocation, or something else?

Deeper speculation soon revealed that recent veiling was not necessarily a "return" to the veil or a retrograde step. Despite superficial similarities between the abandoned veil and the new one, the two were distinguishable and quite different stylistically, symbolically, and sociologically (El-Guindi 1983). Young Egyptian women were not returning to the abandoned traditional dress donned by their grandmothers. Instead, women were increasingly coming to wear what they considered legitimate Islamic dress—*al-ziyy al-Islami*. A first stage of the legitimate Islamic dress is a headscarf covering all of the hair and ordinary but modest (long hem, long sleeves) "Western" clothes. A second stage is a long, wide dress of opaque cloth with long sleeves and a headdress outlining the face and covering the dress at the front and the back down to the waist. A third stage is a face veil, usually made of the same color and cloth as that of the headdress. Women dressed according to this last stage are known as *al-munaqabat* (the face veil is *al-niqab*) as opposed to women dressed in the first and second stages, who are known as *muhagabat*. The majority of veiled Egyptian women today are *muhagabat* rather than *munaqabat*.

Symbolically and sociologically, the traditional veil was elitist and served to distinguish the urban aristocracy from the lower strata, whether urban or rural. Women outside the aristocracy and the urban elite vied to veil as a sign of urbanization and upward mobility. By contrast, the Islamic dress is symbolically and sociologically egalitarian. Presumably identical in style, material, and range of permissible colors, it is intended to erase any social or economic differences among its wearers. In this respect, it is consistent with the egalitarian spirit of the Islamic movement that initially, and in part, had gained momentum as a reaction to the increasingly evident gaps between the haves and the have-nots.

While elevating upper-class urban women from the mainstream of society, the traditional veil also had served to symbolize the exclusion of these women from mundane affairs and public life. By contrast, modern women wearing the Islamic dress, at least early in the movement, showed no signs of wanting to return to the *hareem* or of wanting to give up employment outside the home. On the contrary, data showed that the biggest concentration of "veiled" women was in the practical colleges (medicine, engineering, and pharmacy) of Egyptian universities. It was in these colleges that Islamic groups and the Islamic movement were most active and most assertive. Within Egypt's educational system, students of these colleges are those who earn the highest scores in national secondary school certificate examinations, and these students come to occupy the most highly valued and prestigious professions in the country (El-Guindi 1983).

Within this context, it seemed that rather than returning to the traditional elitist veil or the seclusion of *hareem* life, the new Egyptian woman was educated, professional, nonelitist, yet "Islamically" veiled. Still, the reasons for this situation remained enigmatic. The *shar'* (Islamic law) delineating the proper way Muslim women should dress had been in existence for hundreds of years. Why were Egyptian women, who once had led other Muslim women in their desire for liberation, choosing this time to demonstrate in this conspicuous manner an affirmation of Islamic norms of dress? Why, all of a sudden, was this trend appearing among one of society's most educated sectors—urban college women?

To many the answer lay in the same reasons that had led to the revival of Islamic traditions and codes of conduct as the most viable and appealing alternatives to the existing social order and existing morality. Yet, characterizing the contemporary Islamic movement in Egypt or elsewhere in the Arab world as a "revival" of Islam or as a "resurgence" of Islamic fundamentalism is to some extent erroneous and illusory. What has happened is not so much that sentiments and beliefs have changed, but that the scope of political discourse and activity has widened (Hourani 1983). As a result of the socialist transformation of the Nasser period, many of the actors in the contemporary political process in Egypt and the formulators of ideology are being drawn from a wider social range than ever before. The young men and women studying in universities and entering government service or the professions are coming from a larger area of society. Egypt has never been really secularized. Apart from a Westernized elite, Islam and Islamic traditions and norms of conduct have remained very much alive and part and parcel of the activities of daily living for the majority of Egyptians. As new actors in the political process and in the defining of ideologies, middle- and lower-class Egyptians are bringing to the fore sentiments and behaviors that long have been in existence but that Egyptians are having a chance to assert for the first time.

However, there is more to the contemporary Islamic movement in Egypt than the higher visibility of self-identity in Islamic terms. To the minds of the majority of Egyptians, Westernization is associated with immorality and corruption; thus, to most of the populace, opening economic doors to Western goods also opened the door to moral laxity and social disruption. In the midst of the heightened sense of the difference between Muslims and non-Muslims and the distrust of imported ideas, morality, and codes of conduct, there was an increased respect for the ritual observances of Islam, daily prayers, the annual pilgrimage, and fasting during the month of Ramadan, and a more tenacious holding on to the precepts of Islamic Sharia, not only as a system of laws but also as the repository of moral Islamic values. As a conscious assertion of Islamic identity, there also was an emphasis on certain symbolic acts, such as abstention and abolition of alcohol and the establishment of Islamic non-interest-making banks. Among these symbolic acts the most visible was the wearing of Islamic dress by women (Hourani 1985).

To some women, the wearing of traditional Islamic dress may have been a response to male fundamentalist pressures. However, there is ample evidence that for the majority it was quite voluntary. According to some observers, what distinguishes the Islamic movement in Egypt from Islamic movements elsewhere in the Arab world is the crucial role that Egyptian women are playing in defining the nature, direction, and goals of the movement in Egypt (El-Guindi 1981). One author goes so far as to suggest that the whole Islamic movement in Egypt started as a women's movement that was only later exploited by men for their own purposes (Williams 1980). Whatever the case, what is evident is that Egyptian women are willing and enthusiastic participants in this new trend and style of dressing.

Veiled, educated, professional women of the middle and lower classes represent a complicated response to a complicated world that overwhelms and confuses them. This world includes an influx of foreigners, oil wealth, expensive consumer goods, inflation, and "alien" lifestyles. Clinging to their heritage is women's way of imposing a semblance of order on an otherwise confusing world and their means of restoring self-worth and lessening alienation. Through veiling, women are making a clear statement that they are being quite selective about "modernity" (Ibrahim 1982b). They are taking out of it education and professional careers, the elements consistent with their heritage and Islamic traditions, and they are leaving out all the rest. The Islamic veil thus may be part of a new assertive Islamic movement with a powerful message that synthesizes modernity and authenticity.

Yet, there is more than symbolism to the prominence of women in the contemporary Islamic movement. In societies where secular ideologies and morality are dominant, the issue of the roles and status of women is of minor significance. This is attested to by the fact that despite the extensive literature on capitalism and socialism, very little of it touches on the role of women in society. With the entry of religion into the political debate, morality is at the heart of the political discussion. Especially in traditional societies where religion and religious scriptures are major determinants of the lives of women, the issue of their roles and status acquires political significance and comes to occupy top priority on the agenda of public debate and discussion.

What may indeed have commenced as a trend symbolizing loyalty to Islamic values and traditions and the beginnings of an intelligent and selective synthesis of modernity and authenticity is gradually transforming itself into a call for the "retraditionalization" of women's status and roles and women's return to their "proper" place within the home and within society as a whole. In the summer of 1985, a draft law was presented to the People's Assembly (the Egyptian Parliament) calling for women—notably middle-class, educated women—to quit their jobs while retaining half their salaries. The rationale behind the draft law was that working women were neglecting the care and upbringing of their children, thereby contributing to an increase in the incidence of juvenile delinquency and drug addiction among the young. The presentation of the draft law was followed by a strong media campaign aimed at creating an ideological climate against women working outside the home, which in the process galvanized the debate about the roles and status of women. Journalists, writers, thinkers, and scientists from across the political spectrum were drawn into the debate so that no less than two hundred articles and columns appeared in the national press addressing the topic.

In terms of legal codes and constitutional rights, Egyptian women are losing ground as well. In July 1979, the People's Assembly (following President Sadat's personal initiative) had enacted Law 44 amending the Personal Status Law in effect since 1929. According to the provisions of the new law, a woman had the right to ask for and secure a divorce within one year of her husband's taking on a second wife, hence restricting polygamy to some extent. Also, according to the new laws a divorced woman who had custody of young children was entitled to remain in the marital abode until her children reached the legal age, after which they would live with their father. Although these amendments were nothing compared to what feminists had been demanding for more than a half century, the amendments were considered breakthroughs nonetheless. Also, during the same year and as part of the constitutional reforms following the signing of the March 1979 treaty with Israel—reforms designed to prepare Egypt for a new era of peace— thirty seats in the People's Assembly were reserved for women. This, again, was heralded as a progressive step that would enable women to play a more visible role in the political arena.

Both laws recently were repudiated. In June 1985, the changes made in the Personal Status Law during Sadat's time were ruled unconstitutional and against Islamic Sharia; hence, only the 1929 family laws were valid. New amendments were passed by Parliament, but these were very minor amendments of the 1929 family laws. The constitutional law giving women thirty seats in Parliament was repealed during the 1978 People's Assembly elections.

There is evidence that this call for the "retraditionalization" of the roles of Egyptian women is instigated by the increasing levels of unemployment. University graduates in the thousands are finding it more and more difficult to find jobs. The Ministry of Labor, charged since the late 1960s with employing all university graduates, in only today starting to employ the graduates of 1982 and 1983. The decline of work opportunities in oil-rich Arab countries due to the "oil glut" and the consequent decline in the prices of oil mean that the contracts of at least 1 million Egyptian migrants are being terminated. Increasing numbers of migrants are returning to their home country to seek new employment or to claim the jobs they once vacated. As usually happens in times of rampant unemployment, the most ready answer that seems to offer itself is to send women back to their homes.

On March 19, 1987, two days before Mother's Day, one of Cairo's dailies, *Al-Akhbar,* published a front-page news story with this headline: "Dahmouch is advocating the return of Egyptian women to the *hareem.*" The news story went on to explain that the director general of the General Organization for Textile Industries, Dr. al-Sayed Dahmouch, had issued a decree effective immediately forbidding the employment of women in all Egyptian textile factories. The decree was to apply equally to all levels of employment in the textile industry: factory workers, medical doctors, engineers, and accountants. The decree, announced the newspaper, had been signed by the minister of industry. This news story was later denied by Dahmouch, but not before raising numerous questions and discussions concerning the whole issue of women working outside the home. Whether the law in fact will be applied or not remains to be seen.

The experience of Egyptian women with public life has been complicated and compounded by the absence of support services and the persistence of traditional values concerning women's roles and status. Working outside the home has forced women to cope with double- and multiple-role conflicts and an increased work load. In fact, many women have found the experience subjugating. What is striking in the ongoing mass media debate is that some women at all levels of employment, from professionals, doctors, engineers, and even members of Parliament to factory workers, are themselves advocating that women give up their public roles.

The ongoing debate in Egyptian mass media today on the roles and status of women is reminiscent in several respects of the debate raised almost a century ago by the publication of Qasim Amin's book *The Emancipation of Women.* In both instances, the role of Islam in the modern world was a key issue. In both instances, the debate was ignited by a national crisis— the British occupation in the first debate and a devastating economic crisis in the current one. In both instances, there is a plurality of sociopolitical forces competing for power, their stances on the issue of women dictated by their political ideologies. However, there are two main differences. First, the argument a century ago was whether upper- and middle-class women who were uneducated, veiled, and secluded should be given more education, more public roles, and more freedom. The argument today is quite the reverse—that is, whether Egyptian women, who enjoy extensive civil freedoms, occupy one-third of university seats, and hold one-quarter of professional jobs, should be made to quit their public roles and concentrate only on their traditional roles as mothers and housewives. Second, a century ago women were excluded from the debate. Today, as members of Parliament, as journalists, writers, thinkers, and professionals, women enjoy a comparatively greater visibility in the political arena and in public life. Through jobs, magazines, and organized groups, women play a more prominent role in the creation of their own images and in the formulation of the ideologies that structure their lives and social reality. Which "image" women will choose to propagate and stand by remains to be seen. There is still hope.

Dr. Sohair al-Qalamawy, in Parliament, 1981 (Photograph courtesy of al-Akhbar*)*

· PART THREE ·

Egyptian Feminism Within a Theoretical Framework

CHAPTER SEVEN

Conclusions

A number of theories and approaches have been forwarded to explain the changing roles and status of Arab women, Egyptian women included, and it is to these that I now turn to assess how these theories apply to the history of the Egyptian feminist movement as presented in this book. As mentioned in the introduction, this book has been exploratory and eclectic. Although I wrote it within a theoretical framework that recognized and acknowledged the intricate relationship between the changing roles and status of women and the socioeconomic and political organization of society, I did not select a priori one theory or set of ideas and try to apply it rigidly in the collection of information. The challenge remained to find a dominant trend or an all-encompassing theory that would explain the changing roles and status of Egyptian women across time and class boundaries. This challenge has not been met. Rather what I have found is some support for a number of already existing theoretical approaches. With some qualifications, these approaches can be adequately used to explain the emergence of each phase of the Egyptian feminist movement. In the following analysis I present a phrasing of each of these approaches and then proceed to examine to what extent it coincides with or differs from the experiences of Egyptian women.

• ARAB WOMEN'S MOVEMENTS ARE
DERIVATIVES OF WESTERN WOMEN'S MOVEMENTS •

One approach to the analysis of the changing roles and status of Arab women is the view that the catalyst for these changes was the closer contact of the Arab region with the West. Arab women's history, as part of the history of the region, is perceived as a derivative of the history of the West and determined by the forces of Western penetration. The changes in the roles and status of Arab women therefore are seen as the product of the transfer of Western ideas (see, for example, Baer 1964). Implicit in this analysis is the assumption that the status and roles of women in any society are the product of a set of ideas, whether indigenous or imported (Tucker 1983:324). Women's history thus is shaped predominantly by intellectual currents, and these currents, at least as far as the Arab world is concerned, were dependent on stimulation from the West. Change and evolution in the lives of Arab women began with an intellectual elite acquainted with Western thought that initiated the discussion of women's role in society. This discussion eventually filtered down and took concrete legal and political form.

Egyptian feminism in its first phase, the intellectual debate phase, indeed aimed at the integration of Western-inspired attitudes toward women into an Islamic framework or even the discarding of Islamic attitudes altogether. Yet, although it may be true that the roles and status of women are the product of ideas and internalized values, it also is true that ideas and internalized values, especially those relating to women's roles and status, are the most difficult aspect of any social order to change. As part of Westernization, Egyptian feminism in its first phase remained confined to the upper classes and scarcely made a dent in the consciousness of the other classes of late nineteenth and early twentieth century Egypt. One of the earliest outcomes of the Western (British) penetration of Egypt was the disruption of the moral and cultural continuum between the native upper classes and the rest of the population. Islam was, and still is, the single most unifying element in Egyptian cultural heritage. Islam (or interpretations of Islam) also was the most important single element defining the traditional roles of women. The increased Westernization of the upper classes was paralleled by an intensification of religious fanaticism and xenophobic rejection of non-Islamic ideas, including ideas relating to women, among the other classes of Egyptian society. The deep religiosity of the majority of Egyptian men and women, educated and uneducated, remained the major obstacle to Western-inspired ideas concerning the "emancipation" of women. This religiosity, which defined Egyptians' world view and upheld and explained the social order to which they belonged, was the one factor whose significance was undermined by the intellectual leaders of the Islamic Reform Movement. This religiosity is also the one factor that caught modern analysts unawares when Islam reemerged as a major sociopolitical force in contemporary Egypt. The intellectual debate phase of Egyptian feminism did not bring about any significant changes in the lives of Egyptian women.

• ARAB WOMEN'S MOVEMENTS ARE DERIVATIVES OF NATIONAL LIBERATION MOVEMENTS •

In contrast to approaches that emphasize the transfer of Western ideas to the Arab world as the major catalyst for the birth of indigenous feminist movements, another approach considers women's movements in the region as derivatives of national liberation movements. Especially in the case of Egypt, the women's movement is generally believed to have been born with the nationalist movement to liberate the country from British occupation. Implicit in this approach is the assumption that nationalists and indigenous political leaders sought the liberation of women as an integral part of liberation efforts. For these leaders, the betterment of the social status of all groups of society was inseparable from national independence. The sharpening of collective consciousness and the strengthening of nationalistic feelings called for the support of all sections of the population, including women. In other words, national liberation movements are as liberating for women as for the countries to which they belong.

Between 1919 and 1924, the nationalist phase of Egyptian feminism, Egyptian women played a very prominent role in nationalist activities to oust the British and attain national independence for Egypt. For the first time in Egyptian history, hundreds of veiled upper-class Egyptian women repeatedly flooded the streets of Cairo to protest British policy. Women of other classes also participated in these public protests, and some of them died from British bullets and thereby became national heroines and martyrs. As members of the Wafd, the best organized political party in the annals of Egypt's modern history, Egyptian women further participated in political agitation by boycotting British products and by acting as communication links between imprisoned nationalist heroes and their followers. The nationalist activities of 1919 and the ensuing years led to the liberation of Egypt when in 1922 the British unilaterally declared Egypt's independence. Not so for Egyptian women. Once the dust settled and there was a return to normalcy, Egyptian women were expected to return to their "normal" and "proper" place within their homes and within society at large. The 1924 constitution did not give women suffrage rights and thus once more excluded them from political participation.

The experiences of Egyptian women in the nationalist phase replicated the experiences of other women with national liberation movements. The contradiction between the promise of change during times of crisis and the restoration of tradition after the return to normalcy was experienced by Algerian women after the 1954–1962 Algerian struggle against French colonization; by U.S. women after the American Revolution; and by Russian,

Chinese, and Cuban women during the postrevolutionary periods of socialist transition. In this context, the experiences of Egyptian and other women attest to the resilience of traditional roles and structures and to the frugality of egalitarian change, at least as a result of national liberation movements.

• WOMEN'S MOVEMENTS ARE BORN AFTER NATIONAL LIBERATION MOVEMENTS •

Perhaps a more adequate formulation of the relationship between women's movements and national liberation movements is that women's movements are born *after* national liberation movements have attained their goals. The participation of women in revolutionary movements widens women's horizons, gives women a taste of freedom, and teaches them techniques of organized struggle. Women's participation in these movements seems to empower them to henceforth take stands on issues relating to their own roles and status. During periods of nationalist struggle, women align themselves with men, identify totally with their goals, and are mere appendages to their organizational activities. After nationalist fervor subsides, and especially as a result of the disillusionment women experience at once more being excluded from public and political life, they turn all their efforts to struggling for their own cause.

The women's movement in the United States in the 1700s and early 1800s was a movement in which women aligned themselves with men's movements, in the hope that struggling for others' rights would help women obtain their own. After the civil war, women received a bitter blow when they were excluded from constitutional amendments extending suffrage rights to blacks but not to women. After the 1860s, women's organizations were formed for the purpose of securing suffrage. This brought into full force the first phase of the U.S. women's movement.

The Egyptian feminist movement, in it social activism phase, also was born after the nationalist movement to free the country from British rule subsided. The feminist movement began in 1923 with the establishment of the Egyptian Feminist Union but came into full force only after Egyptian women experienced the disillusionment of being excluded from the electoral laws promulgated as part of the 1924 constitution. After 1924, the mainstream of the women's movement in Egypt began to be more assertive regarding women's rights. Women of the EFU organized, gave speeches, defined issues, and staked claims. As political agitators who openly demanded full suffrage rights for women and the reform of the Personal Status Law, they worked side by side with social feminists who channeled their talents into philanthropic organizations, setting themselves up as monuments to the constructive and creative powers of women. Still other women concentrated on professional development, eschewing political agitation or social work for the time, but consciously or unconsciously laid the foundations for greater numbers of Egyptian women to follow suit. The social activism phase of the Egyptian feminist movement ended in 1952 when all private organizations and groups were co-opted by the regime and many of the welfare activities were taken over by the state.

• THE COMMITMENTS OF ARAB POLITICAL LEADERS ARE CRITICAL TO CHANGE IN WOMEN'S ROLES •

Many studies of the polity and economy of Arab countries, and Third World countries generally, deemphasize the importance of institutions. Written within a theoretical framework sometimes defined as developmentalism, the most important issue these studies emphasize is the key role played by government leaders and policymakers, particularly presidents, in the development and change of their respective countries. Consequently, within the perspective of these studies, the ideological commitments of presidents are rightly viewed as critical to the nature and direction of national development, which directly or indirectly has a great impact on the nature and direction of change in the roles and status of women (Rassam 1984a:7; Rogers 1979).

A "personalist perspective" whose typical focus is on the single decisionmaker downplays or even excludes other factors; this characterizes much of what has been written about postrevolutionary Egypt (Sullivan 1986:7). Although it is possible to exaggerate the importance of presidential commitments and decisions, certainly no observer of postrevolutionary Egypt can deny the crucial role both Nasser and Sadat played in directing the course of Egypt's development during the past three decades. This suggests that an understanding of Nasser's and Sadat's ideologies and the state policies they initiated are critical to an understanding of the changes in the lives of Egyptian women in postrevolutionary Egypt.

The Nasser regime's espousal of socialism ushered in the statist socialist phase of the Egyptian feminist movement. The espousal of socialism by the state implied a commitment to the equality of the sexes, and this phase was termed *statist* because most of the changes that occurred in the lives of Egyptian women were initiated by a series of state laws enacted as part of the attempted socialist transformation of Egyptian society. A new constitution gave women the right to vote and to stand for public office; a new labor code gave them equal pay for equal work; and education laws gave them access to equitable educational opportunities.

Yet, the experiences of Egyptian women with socialism replicated those of women in other societies undergoing socialist transformation. Women's acquisition of constitutional and legal rights did not automatically or spontaneously bring about a change in long-established, internalized values regarding women's roles and status in society. Thus, there were significant but not radical changes in the nature and level of women's involvement in public life. The intended structural changes were met with strong resistance from traditional attitudes regarding a sexual division of labor within the household, in the political arena, and in society at large. One area where traditional values, shared by both men and women, persisted in the face of structural changes was that of women and fertility. The majority of Egyptian women, despite discrimination in other areas, derived respect, sociopsychological rewards, and status from their roles as mothers, and they were not about to deemphasize the only role that gave them a bargaining position in the social structure. The extensive National Family Planning Program launched by the Nasser regime in the 1960s, aimed at reducing fertility levels, failed for several reasons. Not least important of these was resistance from Egyptian women.

The reversal of Egypt's socialist orientation to capitalism and a free enterprise economy during the Sadat regime was to bring about another set of changes in the lives of Egyptian women.

• THE ROLE OF ARAB WOMEN IS A FUNCTION OF THE WORLD CAPITALIST SYSTEM •

The persistence of poverty and backwardness in Third World countries has led some scholars to give serious consideration to the constraints placed on the development of these countries by international factors, especially the world capitalist system. Concerning the roles and status of women, scholars working within this dependency theory argue that the world capitalist system is responsible to a large extent for the "backwardness" of the household. According to this approach, the household functions to maintain women as a reserve labor force, to be put out on the market and withdrawn as needed. This maintenance of this situation helps ease the economic stress and unemployment generated by the recurring cycles of inflation and depression characteristic of all free enterprise economies. When women's labor outside the home is needed, values of sexual equality are propagated. When women's labor is no longer needed, national and religious leaders begin to extol the virtues of women as wives and mothers, and psychologists begin to emphasize the crucial need of a child for a full-time mother (Rassam 1984a; Saffioti 1978).

If this is true of the core capitalist nations, it is even more so for the countries that become dependent on them. In the latter countries, at least in the initial stages of implementation, the reshuffling of their production structures to fulfill the needs of an open-door free enterprise economy exacerbates inequalities between social classes, reduces employment opportunities, and increases the levels of absolute and relative poverty. Under these circumstances, to ease the economic crisis and vacate jobs for unemployed males, women are asked to return to the home. This call for the "retraditionalization" of women's roles is rarely couched in economic terms, but is usually justified on moral, cultural, psychological, or religious grounds. With some deviations, this pattern has been replicated in Egypt.

· Bibliography ·

Abdel Kader, M. Z. 1973. *The Crisis of the Constitution* [Mehnat al-destour]. Cairo: Madbouli (in Arabic).
———. 1964 *Models of Women* [Namazig min al niss'a]. Cairo: Daral Maaref (in Arabic).
Abdel Kader, S. 1971. "Modern and Conservative Egyptian Family Types." M.A. thesis, American University in Cairo.
———. 1973. *The Status of Egyptian Women: 1900–1973.* Cairo: Social Research Center, American University in Cairo.
———. 1984. "A Survey of Trends in Social Science Research on Women in the Arab Region, 1960–1980." In *Social Science Research and Women in the Arab World.* UNESCO, ed., pp. 139–175. London and Dover, N.H.: Francis Pinter.
Abdel Khaleq, G. 1981. "Looking Outside or Turning Northwest? On the Meaning and External Dimension of Egypt's *Infitah,* 1971–1980." *Social Problems* 28, no. 4 (April):394–409.
Abdullah, A. 1985. *The Student Movement and National Politics in Egypt: 1923–1973.* London: Al-Saqi Books.
Adams, C. 1933. *Islam and Modernism in Egypt: A Study of the Modern Reform Movement Inaugurated by Muhammad Abduh.* London: Oxford University Press.
Ahmed, J. M. 1960. *The Intellectual Origins of Egyptian Nationalism.* London: Oxford University Press.
Ahmed, L. 1984. "Early Feminist Movements in Turkey and Egypt." In *Muslim Women.* F. Hussein, ed., pp. 111–125. London: Croom Helm.
Al-Akhbar. October 10, 1971.
Allen, R. M. A. 1974. *The Study of Hadith 'Isa ibn Hisham.* Albany: State University of New York Press.
Al-Qalamawy, S. 1935. *Tales of My Grandmother* [Ahadith jidadti]. Cairo: Matb'at Lajnat al-Ta'lif wal-Tarjama wal-Nashr (in Arabic).
———. 1962. Introduction to *The Effects of The Desert Searcher* [Athar bahithat al-badiya], by Ahmed Hefni Nasef. Cairo (in Arabic).

150

Al-Qazzaz, A. 1977. *Women in the Middle East and North Africa: An Annotated Bibliography.* Middle East Monographs, no. 2. Austin: Center for Middle Eastern Studies, University of Texas.

Al-Yusif, F. 1953. *Memories* [Zikrayat]. Cairo: Maktabit Ros al-Yusif (in Arabic).

Amin, G. 1981. "Some Economic and Cultural Aspects of Economic Liberalization in Egypt." *Social Problems* 28, no. 4 (April):430–441.

Amin, Q. 1901. *The New Woman* [al-mar'ah al-jadidah]. Cairo: N.P. (in Arabic).

———. 1970. *The Emancipation of Women* [Tahrir al-mar'a]. Cairo: Dar al-Ma'arif (in Arabic).

Ammar, H. 1954. *Growing Up in an Egyptian Village.* London: Routledge and Kegan Paul.

Antoun, R. 1968. "On the Modesty of Women in Arab Muslim Villages: A Study in the Accommodation of Tradition." *American Anthropologist* 70, no. 4:671–697.

Assaad, M. B. 1980. "Female Circumcision in Egypt: Social Implications, Current Research and Prospects for Change." *Studies in Family Planning* 11, no. 1:3–16.

Ayrout, H. 1963. *The Egyptian Peasant.* Boston: Beacon Press.

Badran, H. 1972. "Arab Women in National Development." Paper presented to the Seminar on Arab Women in National Development, Arab League, Cairo.

Badran, M. F. 1977. "Huda Sharawi and the Liberation of the Egyptian Woman." Ph.D. dissertation, Oxford University.

———. 1979. "Middle East and North African Women." *Trends in History: A Review of Current Periodical Literature in History* 1, no. 1: 123–129.

Baer, G. 1964. *Population and Society in the Arab East.* New York: Greenwood Press.

———. 1969. *Studies in the Social History of Modern Egypt.* Chicago: University of Chicago Press.

Bahaa el-Din, A. 1970. Introduction to *The Emancipation of Women,* by Qasim Amin. Cairo: Dar al-Ma'arif (in Arabic).

Baker, R. 1981. "Sadat's Open Door: Opposition from Within." In *Social Problems* 28, no. 4 (April):378–385.

Baker, R. W. 1978. *Egypt's Uncertain Revolution Under Nasser and Sadat.* Cambridge, Mass. and London: Harvard University Press.

Balassa, B. 1977. "Towards a Development Strategy for Egypt." In *Policy Reform in Developing Countries.* New York: Pergamon Press.

Banks, O. 1981. *Faces of Feminism—A Study of Feminism as a Social Movement.* New York: St. Martin's Press.

Berkin, C. R., and C. M. Lovett, eds. 1979. *Women, War and Revolution.* New York and London: Holmes and Meier.

Boulding, E. 1976. *The Underside of History: A View of Women Through Time.* Boulder, Colo.: Westview Press.

Bousquet, G. H. 1966. *L'ethique sexuelle de l'Islam.* Paris: Maison Neuve et Larose.

Bullough, V. L. 1973. "Sex Is Not Enough: Women in Islam." In *The Subordinate Sex: A History of Attitudes Toward Women,* pp. 134–153. Urbana: University of Illinois Press.

Buvinic, M. 1976. *Women and World Development: An Annotated Bibliography.* Overseas Development Council.

Casal, L. 1979. "Revolution and *Conciencia*: Women in Cuba." In *Women, War and Revolution.* C. R. Berkin and C. M. Lovett, eds., pp. 183–306. New York and London: Holmes and Meier.

Central Agency for Public Mobilization and Statistics. 1972. *The Egyptian Woman in Twenty Years* [al-marah al-masriya fi 'ishrin aman]. Cairo.

Central Agency for Public Mobilization and Statistics. 1976. *Preliminary Census Data.* Cairo.

Charvet, J. 1982. *Feminism.* London, Melbourne, and Toronto: I.M. Dent and Sons.

Coleman, J. S. 1955. "The Emergence of African Political Parties." In *Africa Today.* C. Grove Haines, ed., pp. 226–227. Baltimore, Md.: Johns Hopkins University Press.

Collver, A., and E. Langlois. 1962. "The Female Labour Force in Metropolitan Areas: An International Comparison." *Economic Development and Cultural Change* 10, no. 4 (July):367–385.

Constitution of the Royal Kingdom of Egypt. Cairo, 1923.

Cooper, E. 1914. *The Women of Egypt.* New York: Frederick A. Stokes.

Coser, L. 1967. *Continuities in the Study of Social Conflict.* New York: Free Press.

Crabbs, J. A., Jr. 1984. *The Writing of History in Nineteenth Century Egypt: A Study in National Transformation.* Detroit, Mich.: Wayne State University Press.

Culver, E. T. 1967. "Women in Islam." In *Women in the World of Religion,* by E.T. Culver, pp. 270–281. New York: Doubleday.

D'Harcourt, Le Duc. 1893. *L'Egypte et les Egyptiens.* [Egypt and the Egyptians]. Paris: E. Plon.

Deeb, M. 1979a. *Party Politics in Egypt: The Wafd and Its Rivals 1919–1939.* London: Ithaca Press for the Middle East Center, St. Antony's College, Oxford.

———. 1979b. "Labor and Nationalist Politics in Egypt: 1919–1945." *International Journal of Middle Eastern Studies* 10:187–203.

Dessouki, A. 1981. "Policy Making in Egypt: A Case Study of the Open Door Economic Policy." *Social Problems* 28, no. 4 (April):410–416.

Diab, F. 1969. "Measuring Public Opinion in Cairo Toward Granting Political Rights to Women." In *Readings in Social Psychology in Arab Countries.* L. Malik, ed. Cairo: Al-Dar Al-Qawmiya lil Tiba'a wal-Nashr.

Doniach, N. S. 1972. *The Oxford English-Arabic Dictionary of Current Usage.* Oxford: Calderon Press.

El-Guindi, F. 1981. "Veiling *Infitah* with Muslim Ethic: Egypt's Contemporary Islamic Movement." *Social Problems* 28, no. 4 (April):465–485.

———. 1983. "Veiled Activism: Egyptian Women in the Contemporary Islamic Movement." *Femmes de la Mediterranee, peuples mediterraneens* 22, no. 23:79–89.

El-Hamamsy, L. 1958. "The Role of Women in the Development of Egypt." *The Middle East Forum* 23 (June):24–28.

———. 1972. "Belief Systems and Family Planning in Peasant Societies." In *Are Our Descendents Doomed? Technological Change and Population Growth.* H. Brown and E. Hutchings, eds., pp. 335–358. New York: Viking Press.

———. 1975. "The Assertion of Egyptian Identity." In *Ethnic Identity in Continuity and Change.* G. DeVos and L. Romanucci-Ross, eds. Palo Alto, Calif.: Mayfield Publishing Co.

El-Malakh, K. 1973. *The Conqueror of Darkness* [Qahir al-zalam]. Cairo: Dar al-Kitab al-Jadid (in Arabic).

El-Sakakiny, W. 1965. *Qasim Amin: 1863–1908.* Cairo: Dar al-Ma'arif (in Arabic).

Esposito, J. 1980. *Islam and Development.* Syracuse, N.Y.: Syracuse University Press.

Evans, R. J. 1977. *The Feminists: Women's Emancipation Movements in Europe, America and Australasia: 1840–1920.* London: Croom Helm.

Fanon, F. 1967. *A Dying Colonialism.* New York: Grove Press.

Farnsworth, B. B. 1979. "Communist Feminism: Its Synthesis and Demise." In *Women, War and Revolution.* C. R. Berkin and C. M. Lovett, eds., pp. 145–165. New York and London: Holmes and Meier.

Fergany, N. 1972. "Egyptian Women and National Development." Paper presented to the Seminar on Arab Women in National Development, Arab League, Cairo.

Flexner, E. 1970. *Century of Struggle.* New York: Atheneum.

Freeman, J. 1975. *The Politics of Women's Liberation.* New York: David McKay.

Gadalla, S. 1968. "Population Problems and Family Planning Programs in Egypt." Paper presented at the Eighth International Congress of Anthropological and Ethnological Sciences, Tokyo.

Gerner, D. J. 1984. "Roles in Transition: The Evolving Position of Women in Arab Islamic Countries." In *Muslim Women.* F. Hussein, ed., pp. 71–99. London: Croom Helm.

Goode, W. J. 1963. "Changing Family Patterns in Arabic Islam." In *World Revolution and Family Patterns,* by W. J. Goode, pp. 87–164. New York: Free Press.

Gusfield, J. 1968. The Study of Social Movements. In *International Encyclopedia of the Social Sciences.* New York: Crowell, Collier and Macmillan.

Haikal, A. 1971. "Some Managerial Problems of Female Employment in the United Arab Republic." M.A. thesis, American University in Cairo.

Haikal, M. H. 1929. *Biographies: Egyptian and Western* [Taragim: Masriya wa gharbiya] Cairo: Matbait Misr (in Arabic).

Hammam, M. 1980. "Women and Industrial Work in Egypt: The Shubra El-Kheima Case." *Arab Studies Quarterly* 2 (Winter):50–69.

Harb, T. 1899. *The Education of Women and the Veil* [Tarbiat al-mar'ah wa al-hijab]. Cairo: Matbaat al-taraqi (in Arabic).

Haviland, H. F. 1981. "Whither Social-Political Development in the Emerging Nations?" *Social Problems* 28, no. 4 (April):347–362.

Hinnebusch, R. A. 1981. "Egypt Under Sadaat: Elites, Power Structure and Political Change in a Post-Populist State." *Social Problems* 28, no. 4 (April):442–465.

Hodgkin, T. 1961. *African Political Parties: An Introductory Guide.* Harmondsworth, Middlesex: P. Smith, Penguin book, rebound.

Hopkins, N. 1981. "Tunisia: An Open-Shut Case." *Social Problems* 28, no. 4 (April): 385–393.

Hourani, A. 1960. *Arabic Thought in the Liberal Age: 1798–1939.* London and New York: Oxford University Press.

———. 1983. "Conclusion." In *Islam in the Political Process.* James P. Piscatori, ed., pp. 226–235. Cambridge: Cambridge University Press.

Ibrahim, S. 1980. "Anatomy of Egypt's Militant Islamic Groups—Methodological Note and Preliminary Findings." *International Journal of Middle Eastern Studies* 12, no. 4 (December): 423–453.

———. 1981. "An Islamic Alternative in Egypt: The Muslim Brotherhood and Sadaat." *Arab Studies Quarterly* 4, nos. 1 and 2:75–93.

———. 1982a. "Oil, Migration and the New Arab Social Order." In *Rich and Poor States in the Middle East.* Malcolm Kerr and El-Sayid Yassin, eds., pp. 17–70.

Boulder, Colo.: Westview Press.

———. 1982b. *The New Arab Social Order: A Study of the Social Impact of Oil Wealth.* Boulder, Colo.: Westview Press; London: Croom Helm.

———. 1982c. "Social Mobility and Income Distribution in Egypt." In *The Political Economy of Income Distribution in Egypt.* Tignor and Abdel Khaleq, eds., pp. 375–434. New York: Holmes and Meier.

Janeway, E. 1971. *Man's World, Woman's Place: A Study in Social Mythology.* New York: Penguin Books.

Johnson, M. D. 1979. "Old Wine in New Bottles: The Institutional Changes for Women of the People During the French Revolution." In *Women, War and Revolution.* C. R. Berkin and C. M. Lovett, eds., pp. 107–145. New York and London: Holmes and Meier.

Kamel, W. H., et al. 1970. "A Fertility Study in Al-Amria." *The Egyptian Population and Family Planning Review* 1, no. 2:83–100.

Kennedy, M. 1981. "Introduction: Open Doors, Transnationals and the Global Division of Labor." *Social Problems* 28, no. 4, April:339–346.

Khafaga, F. 1984. "Women and Labor Migration: One Village in Egypt." *MERIP Reports* (June):17–21.

Korayem, K. 1981. "The Rural-Urban Income Gap in Egypt and Biased Agricultural Pricing Policy." *Social Problems* 28, no. 4 (April):417–430.

Lane, E. W. 1978. *Manners and Customs of Modern Egyptians.* The Hague and London: East-West Publications.

Levy, R. 1965. "The Status of Women in Islam." In *The Social Structure of Islam,* by R. Levy, pp. 91–134. New York: Cambridge University Press.

Lucas, M. A. 1983. "An African Science, A Feminist Science: Epistemology and Technical Problems." Paper presented at the Seminar on Methodology organized by the Association of African Women for Research and Development, Dakar, Senegal.

Maloney, J. M. 1979. "Women in the Chinese Communist Revolution: The Question of Political Equality." In *Women, War and Revolution.* C. R. Berkin and C. M. Lovett, eds., pp. 165–182. New York and London: Holmes and Meier.

Marsot, A. L. S. 1978. "The Revolutionary Gentlewoman in Egypt." In *Women in the Muslim World.* L. Beck and N. Keddie, eds., pp. 261–276. Cambridge, Mass.: Harvard University Press.

Mengin, F. 1823. *Histoire de l'Egypte sous le gouvernement de Mohammed Aly* [The History of Egypt Under the Rule of Mohammad Ali]. Paris: A Bertrand.

Mernissi, F. 1975. *Beyond the Veil: Male-Female Dynamics in a Modern Muslim Society.* Cambridge: Halsted Press Book, Schenkman Publishers.

Mince, J. 1978. "Women in Algeria." In *Women in the Muslim World.* L. Beck and N. Keddie, eds., pp. 159–171. Cambridge, Mass.: Harvard University Press.

Mitchell, J. 1971. *Woman's Estate.* Harmondsworth, Middlesex: Penguin Books.

Nasif, M. H. 1910. *Women's Issues* [Nissayat]. Cairo: The Jarida Press (in Arabic).

Nelson, C. 1973. "Women and Power in Nomadic Societies of the Middle East." In *The Desert and the Sown: Nomads in the Greater Society.* C. Nelson, ed., pp. 43–59. Berkeley: Institute of International Studies, University of California.

———. 1984. "Islamic Tradition and Women's Education in Egypt." In *The World Yearbook of Education.* S. Acker et al., eds., pp. 211–226. London: Nichols.

Oberschall, A. 1973. *Social Conflict and Social Movements*. Englewood Cliffs, N.J.: Prentice-Hall.

O'Neill, W. L. 1969. *The Woman's Movement: Feminism in the United States and England*. London: Allen and Unwin.

Patai, R. 1952. "The Middle East as a Culture Area." *Middle East Journal* 6, no. 1 (Winter):1–21.

———. 1955. "Dynamics of Westernization in the Middle East." *Middle East Journal* 9, no. 1 (Winter):1–16.

———. 1967. *Women in the Muslim World*. New York: Free Press.

Phillip, T. 1978. "Feminism and National Politics in Egypt." In *Women in the Muslim World*. L. Beck and N. Keddie, eds., pp. 277–294. Cambridge, Mass.: Harvard University Press.

Pope, B. C. 1979. "Revolution and Retreat: Upper-class French Women After 1789." In *Women, War and Revolution*. C. R. Berkin and C. M. Lovett, eds., pp. 215–236. New York and London: Holmes and Meier.

Rassam, A. 1984a. "Introduction: Arab Women: The Status of Research in the Social Sciences and the Status of Women." In *Social Science Research and Women in the Arab World*. UNESCO, ed., pp. 1–13. London and Dover, N.H.: Francis Pinter.

———. 1984b. "Towards a Theoretical Framework for the Study of Women in the Arab World." In *Social Science Research and Women in the Arab World*. UNESCO, ed., pp. 122–138. London and Dover, N.H.: Francis Pinter.

Rogers, B. 1979. *The Domestication of Women: Discrimination in Developing Societies*. New York: St. Martin's Press.

Rowbottam, S. 1974. *A History of Women and Revolution in the Modern World: Women, Resistance and Revolution*. New York: Vintage Books.

Rugh, W. 1979. *The Arab Press*. Syracuse, N.Y.: Syracuse University Press.

Saffioti, H. 1978. *Women in Class Society*. New York: Monthly Review Press.

Saleh, S. 1972. "Women in Islam: Their Status in Religious and Traditional Culture." *International Journal of Sociology of the Family* 2:35–42.

Salem, L. M. 1984. *Egyptian Women and Social Change (1945–1919)* [Al-mar'ah al-masriya wal ta'ghor al-ijtimai']. Cairo: Al-Hi'a al-Misriya al-Amma lil Kitab (in Arabic).

Salmon, M. 1979. "Life, Liberty and Power: The Legal Status of Women After the American Revolution." In *Women, War and Revolution*. C. R. Berkin and C. M. Lovett, eds., p. 85–107. New York and London: Holmes and Meier.

Sen, G. 1985. *Development, Crises, and Alternative Visions: Third World Women's Perspectives*. New Delhi: Development Alternatives for Women in a New Era.

Shanawany, H. 1968. "Factors Accelerating Fertility in Egypt." In *Experiences in Family Planning*. Cairo: Egyptian Family Planning Association.

Shouaib, A. K. 1979. *Economic Opening on Trial*. Beirut: N. P.

Smelser, N. J. 1963. *Theory of Collective Behaviour*. New York: Free Press.

Snyder, E. 1979. "The Anatomy of the Women's Social Movement." In *The Study of Women: Enlarging Perspectives of Social Reality*. N. E. Snyder, ed., pp. 13–58. New York: Harper and Row.

Solanis, V. 1967. *S.C.U.M. (Society for Cutting Men) Manifesto*. Olympia Press.

Sullerot, E. 1968. *Histoire et sociologie du travail feminin* [The History and Sociology of Women's Work]. Paris: Societe Nouvelle des Editions Sonthier.

Sullivan E. 1981. "Women and Work in Egypt." *Cairo Papers in the Social Sciences* 4, Monograph 4 (December): pp. 5–44.

———. 1986. *Women in Egyptian Public Life*. Syracuse, N.Y.: Syracuse University Press.

Tomiche, N. 1968. "The Situation of Egyptian Women in the First Half of the Nineteenth Century." In *Beginnings of Modernization in the Middle East*. William R. Polke and Richard L. Chambers, eds., pp. 171–184. Chicago: University of Chicago Press.

Tucker, J. E. 1976. Egyptian Women in the Work Force. *MERIP Reports* 50:3–12.

———. 1979. "Decline of Family Economy in Mid-Nineteenth Century Egypt." *Arab Studies Quarterly* 1, no. 3:245–271.

———. 1983. "Problems in the Historiography of Women in the Middle East: The Case of Nineteenth Century Egypt." *International Journal of Middle Eastern Studies* 15:321–336.

UNESCO. 1970. "The Education of Women in the U.A.R. During the 19th and 20th Centuries," Special report prepared by Hekmat Abu Zeid et al. for UNESCO, Cairo.

Van Dusen, R. 1976. "The Study of Women in the Middle East: Some Thoughts." *Middle East Studies Association Bulletin* 10:1–20.

Vatikiotis, P. 1980. *The History of Egypt from Muhammad Ali to Sadaat*. Baltimore, Md.: Johns Hopkins University Press.

Williams, J. A. 1980. "Veiling in Egypt as a Political and Social Phenomenon." In *Islam and Development*. John Esposito, ed., pp. 71–85. Syracuse, N.Y.: Syracuse University Press.

Woodsmall, R. F. 1956. *Study of the Role of Women: Their Activities and Organizations in Lebanon, Egypt, Iraq, Jordan and Syria*. New York: International Federation of Business and Professional Women.

———. 1975. *Moslem Women Enter a New World*. New York: A.M.S. Press.

Yehia, M. K. 1983. *The Historical Roots for the Emancipation of Egyptian Women in the Modern Age* (Al-gozour al-tariikhiya li-tahrir al-mar'a fi al-asr al-hadith). Cairo: Al-Hi'a al-Misriya al-Amma lil Kitab (in Arabic).

Youssef, N. H. 1971. "Social Structure and the Female Labor Force: The Case of Women Workers in Muslim Middle Eastern Countries." *Demography* 8:427–439.

———. 1974. *Women and Work in Developing Societies*. Berkeley: Institute of International Studies, University of California.

———. 1978. "The Status and Fertility Patterns of Moslem Women." In *Women in the Muslim World*. L. Beck and N. Keddie, eds., pp. 69–100. Cambridge, Mass.: Harvard University Press.

Yusef, S. H. 1965. "In Defense of the Veil." In *The Contemporary Middle East*. B. Rivlia and J. Szyliowicy, eds., pp. 335–359. New York: Random House.

Zurayk, H. 1979. *The Measurement of Women's Economic Participation*. Regional Paper no. 12. Cairo Population Council: West Asia and North Africa.

· Index ·

157